Illustrators

CONTENTS

OFFICERS

Honorary President	Harold Von Schmidt
President	Charles McVicker
Executive Vice President	Les Thompson
Vice President	John Witt
Secretary	Warren Rogers
Treasurer	Dean Ellis
Associate Treasurer	Roland Descombes
House Chairman	Gerald McConnell

ILLUSTRATORS 19 COMMITTEE

Chairman	Howard Koslow
Assistant Chairman	Doug Johnson
Editor of Annual Book	Gerald McConnell
Designer of Annual Book	Eugene Light
Designer of Call for Entries	Milton Charles
Hanging Chairman	Mitchell Hooks
Show Coordinator	Arpi Ermoyan
Staff	Jill Bossert
	Terry Brown
	Anna Lee Fuchs
	Gloria List
	Norma Pimsler

ISBN: 8038·3409·8 • Library of Congress Catalog Card Number: 59-10849 • Printed in the United States of America

Distributors
CANADA: Saunders of Toronto Ltd., Don Mills, Ontario
GREAT BRITAIN: Transatlantic Book Service, Ltd., 7 Maiden Lane, London WC2E 7NA
AUSTRIA, GERMANY, SWITZERLAND: Arthur Niggli Ltd., Bohl, 9052 Niederteufen AR, Switzerland
FRANCE: Editions Paralleles, 172 rue Pelleport, Paris XXe
All other countries: Fleetbooks c/o Feffer and Simons, Inc., 100 Park Avenue, New York 10017

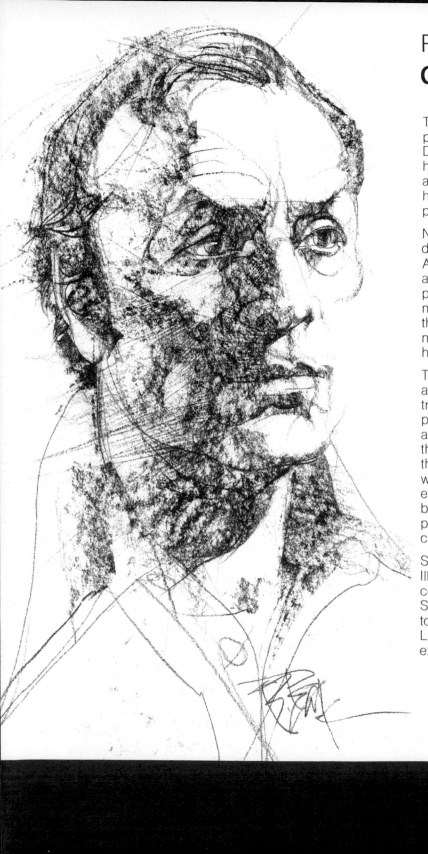

PRESIDENT'S STATEMENT
CHUCK McVICKER

The Illustrators Annual began 19 years ago as a protest against the non-inclusion of art in the Art Directors' Annual. At that time nobody would have had the audacity to even call the Illustrators exhibit and book an annual. But that is what it became. It has survived criticism and boycotts and financial problems.

Now, 19 years later, the Art Directors' Annual still doesn't include much artwork, but the Illustrators Annual is no longer a protest. It is a resounding affirmation of the vitality and creativity of a noble profession. Illustrators, much maligned as "commercial" artists are now making statements within the limitations of their craft which transcend the market place. This book has in its pages art in its highest sense.

The Society of Illustrators, this past year, sponsored an exhibit entitled "200 Years of American Illustration." This show contained almost a thousand paintings covering the period specified and marked an increasing flow of work from the printed page to the museum and gallery. It's my own fondest wish that the efforts of the many artists and supporters who have put so much effort in mounting these exhibits over the years have their endeavors blessed by the greatest recognition of illustration in the pantheon of the arts, and of the illustrator as a truly creative artist.

Special appreciation is due this year to the juries of Illustrators 19, to Chairman Howard Koslow and his committee, to Arpi Ermoyan and the staff at the Society of Illustrators, to Babe Fuchs and Gloria List, to Editor Jerry McConnell and to Designer Gene Light for maintaining the high standards that are expected of this exhibition and book.

19

Leo Dillon has the powerful build of a blacksmith, possesses a booming, infectious laugh and recounts a story with a preacher's facility for oratory.

Diane Dillon moves elegantly, cat-like, remaining quiet until she devastates with a perfect, hilarious one-liner sending Leo's big laugh free.

These are the contrasts that form the totality reflected in their art which is as graphically powerful as it is elegant. Working on each piece together, passing it back and forth in their studio that has twin drawing boards an arm's length apart, they stimulate, help and keep one another growing.

The cohesive element of their dissimilar personalities is the uncompromising desire to produce their illustrations on their own terms, to have pleasure doing so and to utilize different techniques to solve each problem. The result is an incredibly varied portfolio that ranges from watercolor and pastel to wood carving and stained glass. Because of their practice of coming up with a totally new approach for each project, the Dillons hit on solutions far superior to what their clients' could have imagined.

After graduating from Parsons School of Design where they met as students of John Groth and Leo Leonni, they began the partnership that, in the early years, resulted in illustrations for publications such as *Ladies' Home Journal* and *The Saturday Evening Post*. A delightful yield of this partnership is Lee, their handsome, articulate, charmingly self-possessed, eleven-year old son.

In recent years they have collaborated almost exclusively on children's books, two of which earned them the prestigious Caldicott Medal in 1975 for *Why Mosquitoes Buzz in People's Ears*, and in 1976 for *Ashante to Zulu*, the cover of which being this year's Hamilton King selection. Their efforts have been rewarded with recognition from *The Boston Globe* for *Song of the Boat* in 1965, the Hugo, for best illustration in the Science Fiction field for a series of covers they did for Ace Books in 1971, several Children's Book Showcase Awards and *The New York Times* Best Books for 1976.

Currently on the board are: a children's book for Dial, a volume of poetry for Crowell and what promises to be a lyrically beautiful book for Little Brown.

The Dillons have become popular lecturers in schools up and down the East Coast and for good reason; utterly fascinating as individuals, they are totally fascinating as a working couple who produce rich illustration that is as skillful as it is enchanting.

Jill Bossert

Known to his closest friends as "Geissmann," Bob died on October 12, 1976,
leaving behind many accomplishments
for which he will long be remembered.

Geissmann was born August 18, 1909 in
New Washington, Ohio. He went to High
School in Warren, Ohio, where he played
football with such ferocity that he was
made a cheerleader. After graduation,
he ran a printing business in the base-
ment of his home and taught art at
Warren Jr. High School for a semester.
At the end of that year, he enrolled at Ohio
State University to study art and design
for three years. Upon leaving Ohio State,
he went to work for Fawn Art Studios in
Cleveland, later moving to Charles E.
Cooper Studio in New York, where his
career really began. He left Cooper Studio
to free lance, and shortly thereafter mar-
ried Merry Whitcomb, an innovator in the
fashion world and sister of Jon Whitcomb,
the most successful and prominent illustrator of that day. During the early forties,
Merry and Geissmann had a son, Christopher, who now teaches college. When the
War began, Geissmann worked with a
group of illustrators in the graphics design
division of the War Department, and it
was while working there that he made
contacts with the Air Force which later
blossomed into the Illustrators Air
Force Program.

It seems only natural that Geissmann,
with his great talent and charm, would
gravitate to the Society of Illustrators as
he did. Most members are familiar with
his work on the ethics committee, the
annuals, the Girlie Shows, his Presidency
of the Society and the myriad committees
on which he served.
Some of his other accomplishments how-
ever, were a bit more unusual. Few
remember that at one time, what is pres-
ently the Bar, was the Library, a room
lined with too many books, a huge
Baroque Oak Table, a few chairs; the
whole thing a bit dingy. Geissmann moved
the Library upstairs, designed a Bar and
Back Bar, covered the walls with felt,
designed a chandelier, put up louvered
folding doors, and lo, we improved the
Library and acquired a new Bar. Those
wood carved nymphs and cherubs inlaid
in the front of the Bar were once the legs
from a Library Table owned by Charles
Dana Gibson.

For his many years of extraordinary and
unique devotion to the Society of Illustrators, the Editors of the 19th Illustrators
Annual wish to dedicate this edition to the
memory of Geissmann. He was our
President, our Benefactor; he was our
Friend.

Bill Kammer

IN MEMORIAM
ROBERT GEISSMANN
1909-1976

HALL OF FAME 1977
ROBERT PEAK

There is an adage that an advertisement is only good if it sells. Hollywood, for example, is conscious of its need to attract the audience to the marquees first. Magazines, too, see this need to capture attention through their use of innovative artwork. Since the mid-1950's, art directors have recognized that Bob Peak's illustrations do these things. The list of his clients is extensive and reflects the versatility of his talent to bring eye-catching appeal to the product. With several techniques in his repertoire, each pains-takingly perfected, he is always able to bring a fresh approach to a subject.

Born in Denver, Colorado in 1928, Bob spent his early years in Kansas and later earned an art degree from Wichita State University. After his military service, he also received a degree from the Art Center College of Design in Los Angeles. By this time his technical skill was evident and attracted a lucrative campaign from Old Hickory Whiskey. This was soon after his arrival in New York. The exposure, appearing weekly on the back covers of Life and Look, led to numerous assignments for Esquire, American, Cosmopolitan and other magazines. He continued to build a reputation in the advertising field with his illustrations for Puritan Sportswear, TWA, Coca-Cola, Owens-Illinois and Schaefer Beer.

In the 1960's, Bob's career flourished. The Artists Guild of New York named him "Artist of the Year" in 1961. This prestigious award, having originated the previous year, honors the top illustrators of the day. The Society of Illustrators Annual Exhibition has included Bob's work in each of its shows since the first exhibition in 1959 and he has been a frequent award winner. A member of the Society since 1961, he received their Hamilton King Award in 1968.

With over forty movie posters to his credit since he illustrated his first, West Side Story, in 1960, Bob has earned a Gold Medal (Camelot, Illustrators 10) and an Award of Excellence (Mame, Illustrators 17). My Fair Lady, Rollerball, The Missouri Breaks, Islands in the Stream and The Spy Who Loved Me are some of the other films for which he has produced the poster art.

The Peaks lived in a spacious studio on New York's Central Park South for several years before moving in 1963 to Greenwich, Connecticut. At first Bob worked in his personally designed studio there but later opened a studio in Westport. In 1976, the Illustrators Workshop was formed by Bob and fellow artists Alan E. Cober, Mark English, Bernie Fuchs, Bob Heindel and Fred Otnes. This unique study program offers intensive instruction sessions and seminars each summer.

Bob's love of motion is easily seen in his art. He received an Award of Excellence (Illustrators '64) for a piece in Sports Illustrated which depicted the speed and power of Pro Football and he has often incorporated sports action into his advertising and editorial work. His hobby, building classic sports cars, grew into a business venture in the early 1970's, but was given less and less attention as it distracted him from his true vocation.

Walt Reed recently wrote in an article in North Light that: "Bob's hallmark has always been his ability to innovate, to present an unusual, arresting and dramatic aspect of an idea." His many exquisite techniques allow him the freedom to innovate. More than an artist of a singular style, he grows as he masters new perspectives and new dimensions. For Bob Peak has risen above the common preoccupation with style alone to concentrate on the artist's real function which he states simply: "Can it Fly?" His successful career answers this question affirmatively.

Terry Brown

WALLACE MORGAN

That the Society of Illustrators in its 76th year can operate from a spacious, well-located townhouse is due in no small measure to the foresight and leadership of Wallace Morgan. It was his (and C. D. Williams') idea to bring the loose knit group of artists, who met irregularly in one of several New York restaurants, together for a monthly smoker (tobacco supplied). As an outgrowth of the smoker, the Artists and Models Show followed and in the late 20's hit Broadway under the Shubert Brothers banner. The royalties it produced fulfilled Morgan's dream of a permanent headquarters for the Society, at first, a blacksmith shop on 24th Street and in 1939 its present digs on East 63rd Street. He served as President from 1929 to 1936 and was an active voice for many years thereafter.

Wallace Morgan was a very prolific artist whose works depicting the human condition showed spontaneity and zest. His subjects, taken from all strata of society, were drawn with humor and compassion and a knowledge of the characteristics of each. He most often worked in charcoal but also did some pen and ink and color wash illustrations. A free hand artist, he never used photography. As he put it: I'll be

damned if I'll use a camera...Besides, they never do me justice."

Born in New York City in 1873, Morgan, whose father was an art instructor, attended classes for six years at the National Academy. In his 20's, he was a staff artist on several New York newspapers including: The Sun, The Herald and the Telegram. His quick sketch style and keen eye for characters were perfected during these years. Later, during World War I, while serving in the AEF as an official artist in the company of Charles Dana Gibson, Jack Sheridan and C. B. Falls, he produced volumes of sketches of battles, Generals and the soldier's day to day routine.

Julian Leonard Street, one of the best known authors of the early 1900's, called upon Morgan to accompany him on his travels which were to be serialized in *Collier's Weekly. Abroad at Home* appeared during 1914 and *American Adventures* during 1917. He also illustrated *The Red Cross Girl*, one in a series by Richard Harding Davis. The other Davis volumes had been illustrated by the likes of Christy, Gibson, Gruger and Emerson.

Morgan was quite active in other New York organiza-

tions as a member of The Players, Century and Dutch Treat Clubs. He was made an honorary member of the Art Students League where he had taught for several years and in 1947 was elected to the National Academy of Design.

An active artist even in his later years, Morgan illustrated a noteworthy series for Carstairs Whiskey in 1947. He died the following May at the age of 75.

This touching report of a memorial exhibition appeared in the *Illustrators Bulletin*, January 1950:

Wallace Morgan's gentleness, his heart and humor, are still with us. Take a walk over to the Faragil Galleries and you'll see Wally. The reason his art is great is because it is a clear, pure expression of the man we all loved. His culture was too ingrained to reach for mannered style, and his intellect too profound to stoop to a quick quip. Just as he spoke with sparkling wisdom—so his art speaks today—and will continue to speak.

JOSEPH CHRISTIAN
LEYENDECKER

(1874-1951)

J. C. Leyendecker, during the first half of the 20th Century, created an image of the American male to match the girls of Charles Dana Gibson, James Montgomery Flagg and Harrison Fisher. The Arrow Collar Man, that thoroughbred sophisticate with a life-style of an F. Scott Fitzgerald character, was well known and well loved, receiving more mail than the screen idols of the day. Leyendecker's enthusiasm for his work and painstaking devotion to perfection are evidenced in the vast amount of advertising, magazine and book illustrations he created, each re-searched, resketched and reworked to his total satis-faction. His life is just one of the many success stories of immigrants to America whose dedication, drive and ability took them to the top of their professions.

Born Joseph Christian, March 23, 1874 in Montabour, a small town in southwestern Germany, he was the eldest of Peter and Elizabeth Leyendecker's three children. The Dutch family immigrated to America in 1882, settling in Chicago where Peter went to work in the family brewery. J. C's art talent surfaced early and after graduating from high school he apprenticed to J. Manz and Company, a Chicago engraving house. For the next seven years he attended classes at the Art Institute of Chicago under John H. Vanderpoehl. Frank, J. C's brother and close friend for many years, joined him for several evening classes. By 1896, enough money had been raised from J. C's salary and his first prize in the *Century* magazine poster contest, for further studies in Paris at the Academie Julian.

J. C., considerably younger than the rest of the students, enjoyed great success in Paris, monopo-lizing the monthly "best artwork" award from the Academie's Adolfe Boureguereau and exhibiting a one man show at the Salon Champs du Mars. At home, his monthly covers, mailed from Paris, for Chicago's *Inland Printer,* began to bring him national attention.

An established craftsman and technician with a warm feeling for human nuance, J. C. had developed a bold stroke and use of color. He maintained a vast collection of his sketches which he used to add details to his work and often painted in color knowing that the piece would be reproduced in black and white.

After three years in Chicago, where J. C's Ivory Soap ads and his first Post cover were completed, the brothers opened a studio near New York's Wash-ington Square. In 1905, J. C. received his most lucrative assignment. Cluett, Peabody and Company, manufacturers of Arrow detachable collars, used J. C's work for the next 25 years, giving him a free hand to create the image of the well mannered gentleman for their campaigns. For models he used some of the aspiring actors of the day and in particular, Charles Beach. The very handsome, square-featured Beach became J. C's lifelong friend, house manager and business aide.

The financial success of the Arrow ads, as well as ads for other clothing manufacturers, and his many magazine covers gave J. C. the freedom to live in luxury. The Washington Square home gave way to the Mt. Tom Road estate in New Rochelle in 1914. Frank, sister Augusta and Charles Beach moved into the new home, which included an elaborate garden and fountain. J. C. maintained a studio near Bryant Park until 1920.

By 1923, a feud between the brothers, which had

been growing for years, caused Frank and Augusta to leave Mt. Tom Road. Frank, who had been disenchanted for many years because he was "the second Leyendecker" and because his penchant for the fine arts was constantly squelched by his brother, died soon afterwards.

J. C.'s magazine work flourished between the Wars even though the depression took its toll on his advertising clients. He became synonymous with the holiday covers for the *Saturday Evening Post* (the New Year's baby and the Thanksgiving turkey) and also illustrated for *Life* and *American Weekly*. His work began to appear in color and, as with Parrish and Pyle earlier, gave full flower to his illustrations.

Financially barely able to hold on to the Mt. Tom Road home after World War II, the 77 year old artist was still actively seeking work when he died of a heart attack on July 25, 1951. At his side was Charles Beach, to whom he left half the estate.

Today, many years after the peak of his fame, one still sees artists emulating J. C. Leyendecker's style. But capturing his strength of design, his technical facility for light and shadow, shape and texture is rare indeed. He blended his talent and training with opportunity to create the artwork which affected Americans for decades.

Terry Brown

Illustrators

CHAIRMAN'S STATEMENT
HOWARD KOSLOW

As one exhibition is put to rest and the resultant art work becomes the Illustrators Annual Book, the next annual show is already taking form. Continuity is the message; continuity must be maintained in order for us to keep before the art buyers and the public the very best in illustration that is created each year. The importance of this showcase of illustration should not be underestimated.

To have participated in helping to maintain the flow from Illustrators #18 to #20 has been a most rewarding experience. Contributing to this accomplishment were many people; the ever efficient staff of the Society and numerous distinguished artists and art directors.

EDITOR'S STATEMENT
GERALD McCONNELL

The task of editing the Illustrators 19 Annual Book was made decidedly easier by my good fortune in obtaining the services of one of the most professional designers I've had the pleasure of working with: to wit, Gene Light. It is, after all, the designer who does 99% of all the work on this book and Gene did it beautifully, promptly and problem-free.

DESIGNER'S STATEMENT
GENE LIGHT

When Gerry McConnell, Chuck McVicker, Arpi Ermoyan and I were discussing the designing of *Illustrators 19*, they said it would be a lot of work.

I said it would be an honor.

They were right—it is a lot of work.

I, too, was right—it is an honor, and I thank the Society for it.

19

JURIES

ADVERTISING:
Robert Shore. Chairman:
Ken Sneider.
Alan Magee.
Linda Holiday.
Alan E. Cober.
Kim Whitesides.
Jim Jonson.
Harry Diamond

EDITORIAL:
Walter Brooks. Chairman:
Bruce Hall.
Ralph Pereida.
Diane Dillon.
Jerry Pinkney.
Seymour Chwast.
Jim Sharpe.
Roger Kastel.
Robert Schulz

BOOK:
Robert Cuevas. Chairman:
Clem McCarthy.
Sandy Huffaker.
Isadore Seltzer.
Bob Ziering.
Burt Silverman.
Roy Andersen

INSTITUTIONAL:
Mark English. Chairman:
Bob Cox.
Jack Thurston.
Betty Fraser.
Robert Giusti.
Reynold Ruffins.
Lou Glanzman

FILM:
Harry Bennett. Chairman:
Joe Csatari.
Gail Ash.
Murray Tinkelman.
Fred Mason

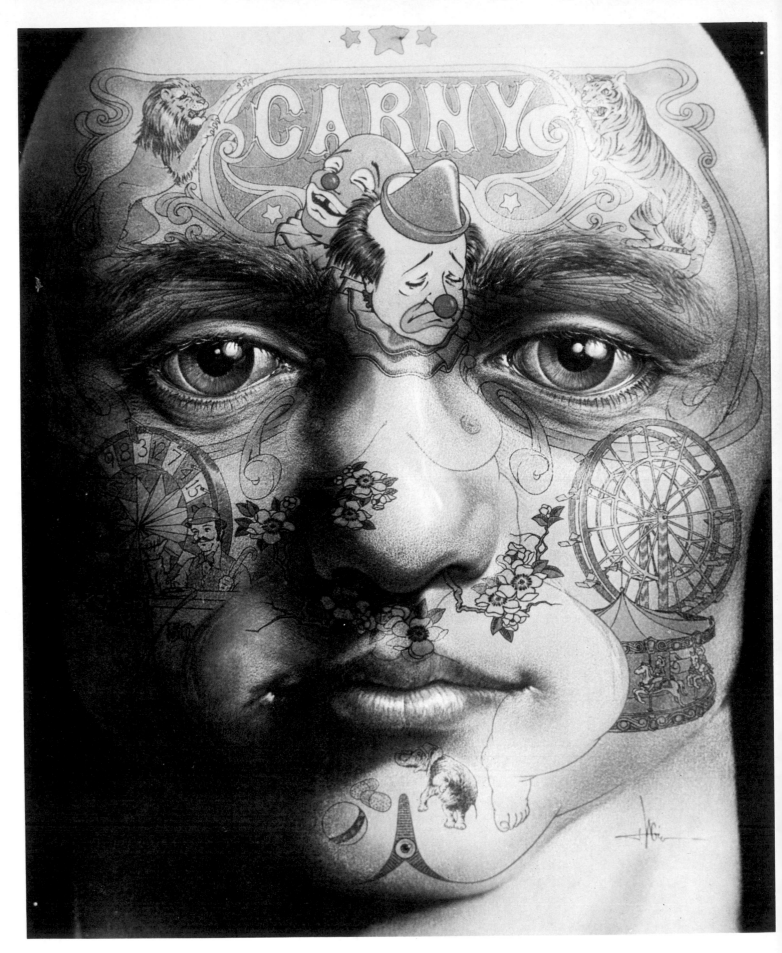

2 Editorial
Artist: **Kunio Hagio**
Art Director: Arthur Paul
Publication: Playboy
Gold Medal

3 Book
Artist: **Candace Walters**
Art Director: Candace Walters

4 Editorial
Artist: **Ted CoConis**
Art Director: Linda Cox
Publication: Cosmopolitan

5 Advertising
Artist: **Babette Marchand**
Art Director: Caroline Redden
Agency: Shaller Rubin Associates, Inc.
Client: Biagi, Division of Swank, Inc.

6 Book
Artist: **Ron Becker**
Art Director: James Plumeri
Title: The Weekend Gardener
Publisher: New American Library

7 Editorial
Artist: **Bob Peak**
Art Director: Jerry Alten
Publication: T.V. Guide

8 Editorial
Artist: **Bernard Fuchs**
Art Director: Richard Gangel
Publication: Sports Illustrated

10 Institutional
Artist: **John Dyess**
Art Director: Jim Barry
Agency: Maritz Motivation
Client: Rolls Royce

9 Advertising
Artist: **George Porter**
Art Director: George Porter
Award for Excellence

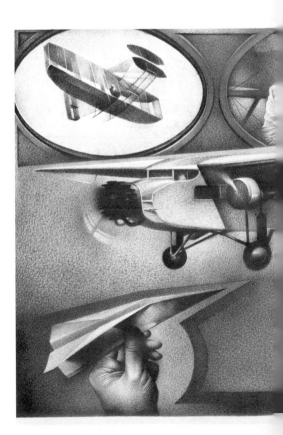

12 Advertising
Artist: **Peter Schauman**
Art Director: Tony Apilado
Agency: John Paul Itta
Client: Evenflo

13 Institutional
Artist: **Dave Warren**
Art Director: Dave Warren

11 Advertising
Artist: **Jack Endewelt**
Art Director: Barbara Gilbert
Agency: Gilbert Associates
Client: Gilbert Associates

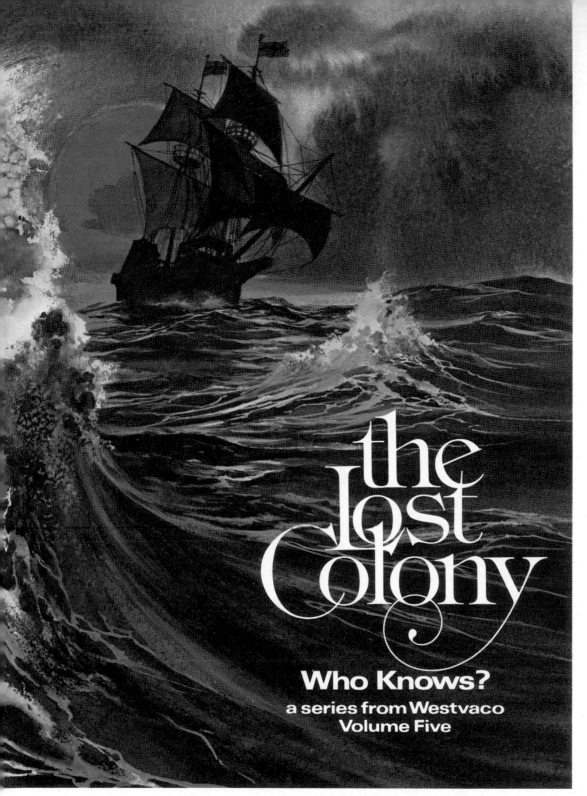

14 Book
Artist: **Harry J. Schaare**
Art Director: Mike Palombo
Title: Who Knows, Vol. 5
Publisher: Westvaco

15 Book
Artist: **Robert Byrd**
Art Director: Robert Kraus
Title: Bridge of Sighs
Publisher: Windmill Books

16 Advertising
Artist: **Andy Warhol**
Art Director: Ria Lewerke
Client: United Artists Records

18 Television
Artist: **Jim Campbell**
Art Director: Dolores Gudzin
Client: NBC Television

17 Television
Artist: **Barbara Nessim**
Art Director: Dolores Gudzin
Client: NBC Television

19 Advertising
Artist: **Gerry Gersten**
Art Director: Marilyn Hoffner
Client: The Cooper Union

21 Advertising
Artist: **Mark English**
Art Director: Jack O'Grady
Client: Jack O'Grady Galleries, Inc.

DONALD BYRD

Caricatures

20 Advertising
Artist: **Al Hirschfeld**
Art Director: Ria Lewerke
Client: United Artists Records

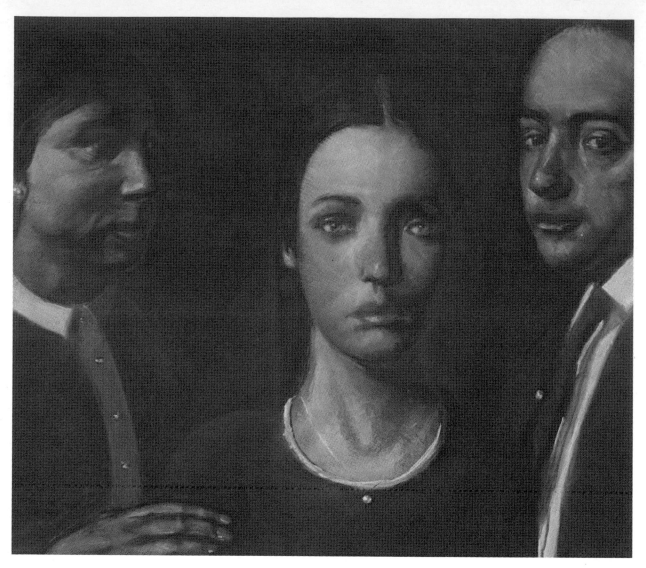

22 Editorial
Artist: **John Collier**
Art Director: Forbes Linkhorn
Publication: American Journal of Nursing
Award for Excellence

23 Book
Artist: **John Thompson**
Art Director: Skip Sorvino
Title: Liquid Trap
Publisher: Scholastic Book Services
Award for Excellence

FOR THE FIRST TIME
THE ORIGINAL AND AUTHENTIC ESCAPES
FROM THE PRIVATE NOTEBOOKS OF
THE WORLD'S GREATEST ILLUSIONIST
Never performed, but always a spectacular
idea in the forefront of his plans...
The Death-Defying Niagara Falls Escape!
Plus The Fantastically Dangerous Under-Water
Escapes—and The Incredible Buried Alive Escape!

24 Book
Artist: **Sanford Kossin**
Art Director: Leonard Leone
Title: Houdini's Escapes
Publisher: Bantam Books, Inc.

25 Book
Artist: **Marc Glessner**
Art Director: Jack Looney
Title: Roles and Relationships
Publisher: Bantam Books, Inc.

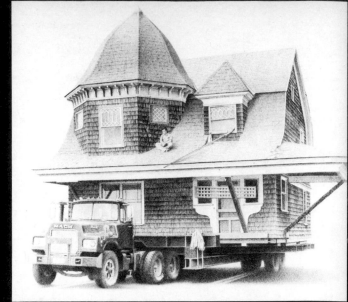

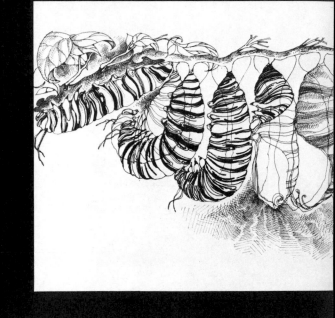

32 Institutional
Artist: **Alan E. Cober**
Art Director: Bo Costello
Agency: Willis/Case/Harwood
Client: Mead Paper
Award for Excellence

33 Book
Artist: **Chet Jezierski**
Art Director: Gene Light
Title: A Class Act
Publisher: Warner Books

35 Advertising
Artist: **Pat Michener**
Art Director: Pat Michener

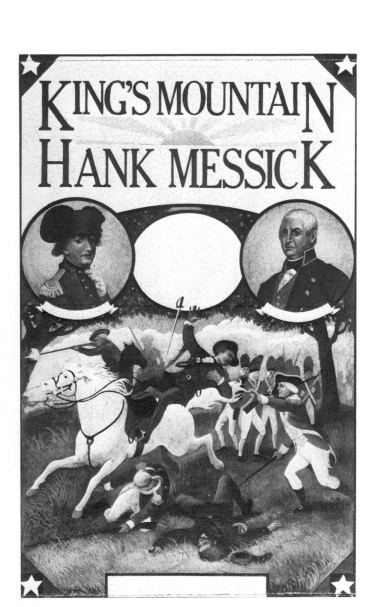

34 Book
Artist: **Wendell Minor**
Art Director: Char Lappan
Title: King's Mountain
Publisher: Little, Brown and Company

36 Editorial
Artist: **Dennis Luzak**
Art Director: Dennis Luzak

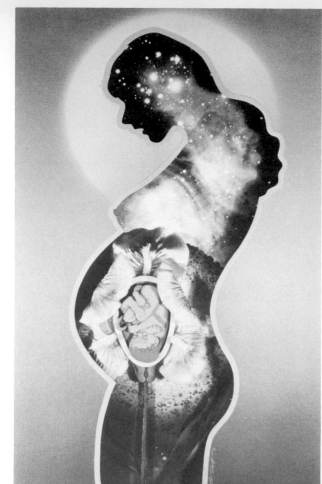

37 Book
Artist: **San Julian**
Art Director: John Van Zwienen
Title: Buck Colter
Publisher: Dell Publishing Co.

39 Book
Artist: **Etienne Delessert**
Art Director: Etienne Delessert
Title: Thomas Et l'Infini
Publisher: Gallimard Publishing

40 Editorial
Artist: **Mitchell Hooks**
Art Director: Joe Sapinsky
Publication: Woman's Day Magazine

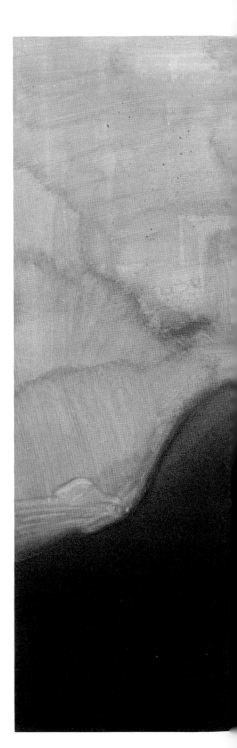

41 Advertising
Artist: **Ronald Williams**
Art Director: Ronald Williams

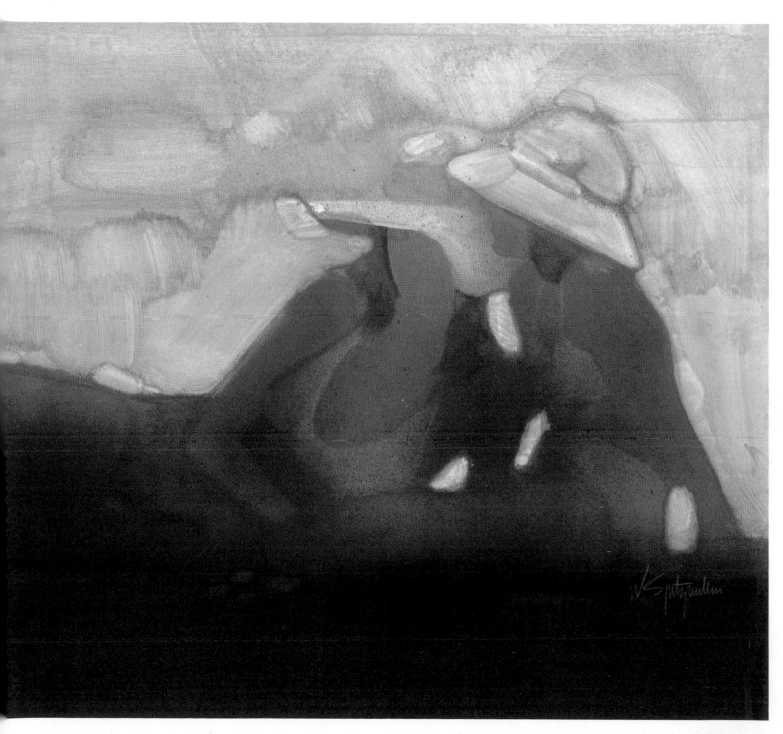

42 Institutional
Artist: **Walt Spitzmiller**
Art Director: Walt Spitzmiller
Client: Keeler/Morris

43 Editorial
Artist: **Saul Lambert**
Art Director: Richard Gangel
Publication: Sports Illustrated

44 Television
Artist: **Gary Soszynski**
Art Director: Gary Soszynski
Client: Infants of Infinity

45 Advertising
Artist: **David Wilcox**
Art Director: Bob Defrin/Abie Sussman
Client: Atlantic Records

47 Advertising
Artist: **Daniel Maffia**
Art Director: Henrietta Condak
Client: CBS Records

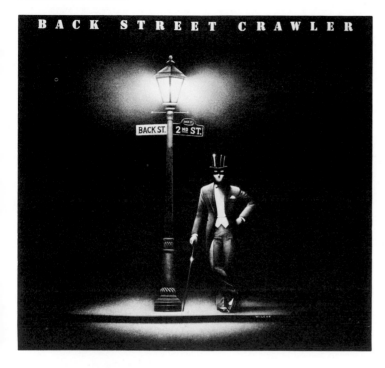

46 Advertising
Artist: **Daniel Maffia**
Art Director: Henrietta Condak
Client: CBS Records

48 Advertising
Artist: **Edward Soyka**
Art Director: Ed Lee
Client: CBS Records

49 Institutional
Artist: **Wilson McLean**
Art Director: Len Fury
Agency: Corporate Annual Reports, Inc.
Client: St. Joe Minerals Corp.
Award for Excellence

51 Television
Artist: **Ted CoConis**
Art Director: Roxanne Edwards
Client: ABC Television

52 Advertising
Artist: **Lorraine Fox**
Art Director: Ken Lavey/David Frank
Agency: Lavey/Wolff/Swift, Inc.
Client: Beecham Laboratories

53 Editorial
Artist: **Matthew G. Roberts**
Art Director: Tae Cara Lon
Publication: Fornacarium Tapes

54 Institutional
Artist: **Thom Ricks**
Art Director: Thom Ricks

55 Book
Artist: **Joanne L. Scribner**
Art Director: Bruce W. Hall
Title: The Witch's Egg
Publisher: Dell Publishing Co.

56 Advertising
Artist: **Reynold Ruffins**
Art Director: Reynold Ruffins
Client: Charles Scribner's Sons

57 Advertising
Artist: **Jerry Pinkney**
Art Director: Ace Lehman
Client: RCA Records

58 Advertising
Artist: **Stephen Durke**
Art Director: John Heck/Jay Loucks
Agency: Weekley & Penny
Client: Houston National Bank

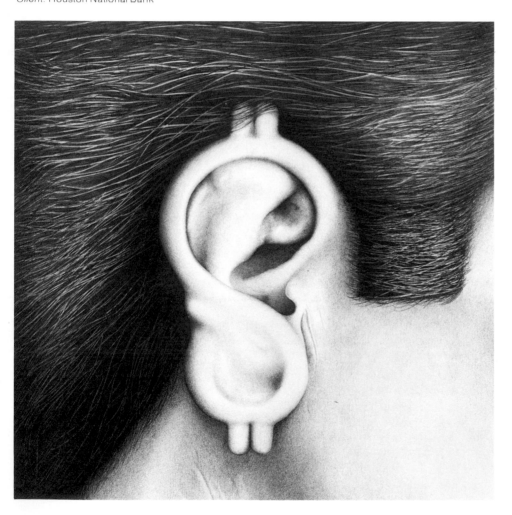

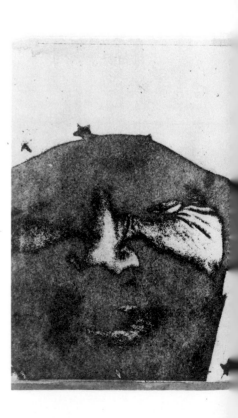

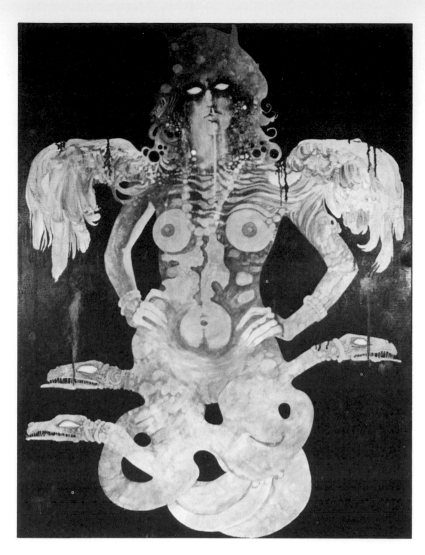

59 Book
Artist: **Ted CoConis**
Art Director: Kristen Schleicher
Publisher: Graphics International

61 Institutional
Artist: **Norman MacDonald**
Art Director: Henry Steiner
Agency: Graphic Communication
Client: Hong Kong & Shanghai Bank

60 Advertising
Artist: **Jane Sterrett**
Art Director: Jane Sterrett

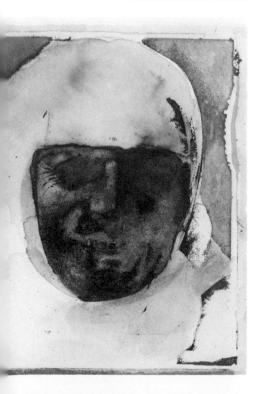

62 Editorial
Artist: **Walt Spitzmiller**
Art Director: Modesto Torre/Alvin Grossman
Publication: McCall's Magazine

63 Editorial
Artist: **Richard Sparks**
Art Director: Bob Feldgus
Publication: Banana Magazine

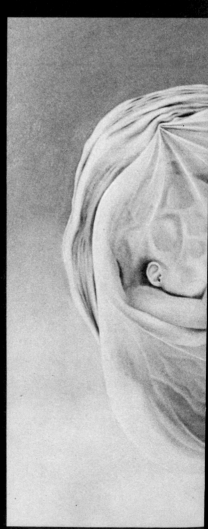

66 Institutional
Artist: **Rich Grote**
Art Director: Rich Grote

67 Editorial
Artist: **Barron Storey**
Art Director: Wade Hancock
Publication: Time Magazine

68 Advertising
Artist: **Jane Sterrett**
Art Director: Jane Sterrett

70 Editorial
Artist: **Louis S. Glanzman**
Art Director: Howard E. Paine
Publication: National Geographic Magazine

69 Book
Artist: **William Downey**
Art Director: Lidia Ferrara
Title: Hal Borland's Book of Days
Publisher: Alfred A. Knopf

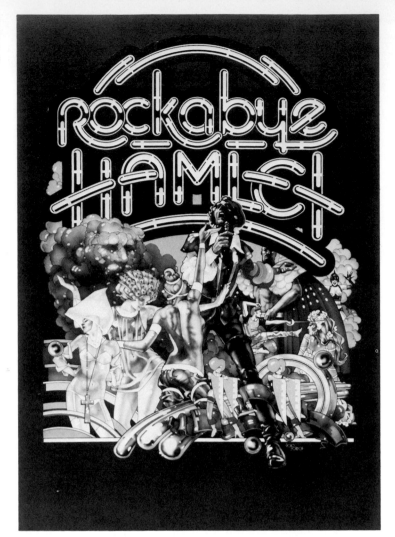

71 Advertising
Artist: **Doug Johnson**
Art Director: Doug Johnson
Client: Leonard Osterman Productions

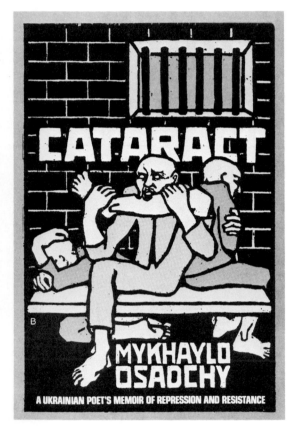

72 Book
Artist: **Barbara Bascove**
Art Director: Harris Lewine
Title: Cataract
Publisher: Harcourt Brace Jovanovich, Inc.

73 Editorial
Artist: **Brad Holland**
Art Director: Steve Heller
Publication: The New York Times

74 Book
Artist: **Robert Heindel**
Art Director: William Gregory
Title: Psycho
Publisher: Reader's Digest

75 Advertising
Artist: **Carol Inouye**
Art Director: Howard Imhoff
Agency: Doremus Advertising
Client: Dime Savings Bank of New York

76 Institutional
Artist: **Etienne Delessert**
Art Director: Etienne Delessert
Client: Musée Des Arts
Gold Medal

78 Book
Artist: **Tim & Greg Hildebrandt**
Art Director: Ian Summers
Title: Clive
Publisher: Ballantine Books, Inc.
Gold Medal

79 Book
Artist: **William Edwards**
Art Director: Leonard Leone
Publisher: Bantam Books

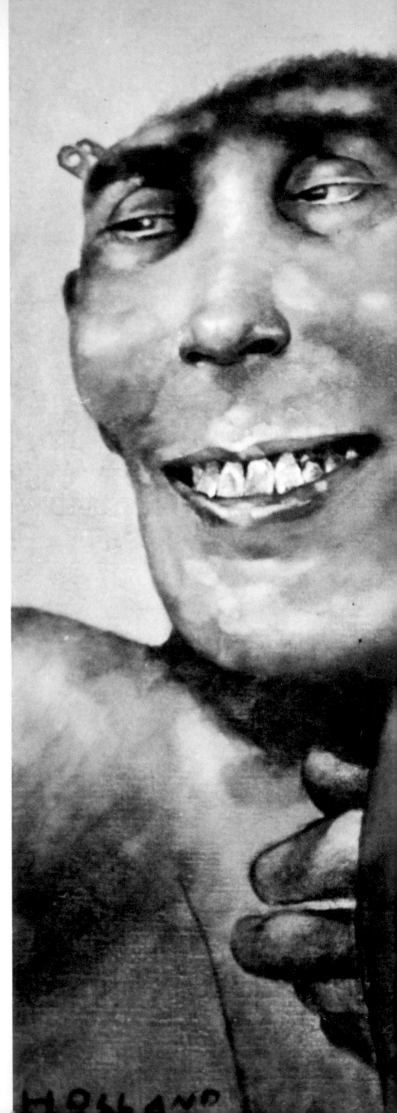

80 Editorial
Artist: **Brad Holland**
Art Director: Arthur Paul
Publication: Playboy
Award for Excellence

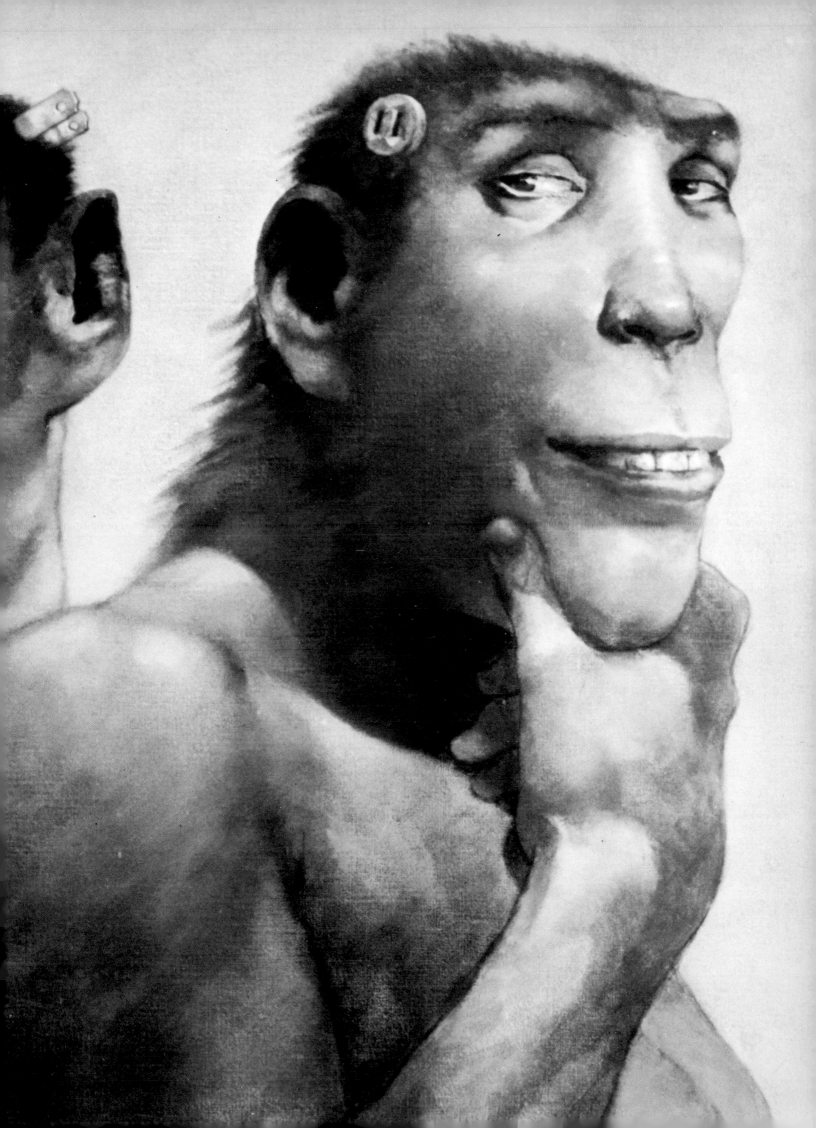

81 Advertising
Artist: **Janet Mager**
Art Director: Bob Heimall
Client: Arista Records

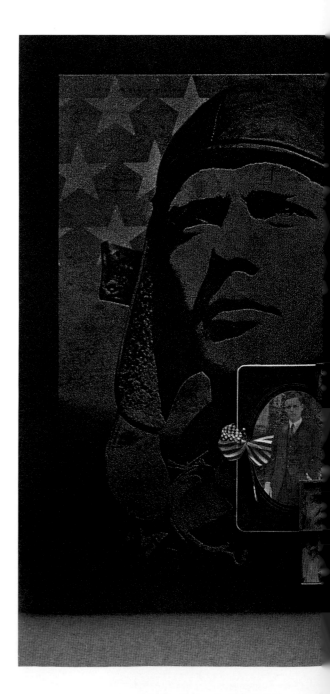

Gen. William "Billy" Mitchell, much-decorated flying ace of World War I and early exponent of air power.

83 Television
Artist: **Charles McVicker**
Art Director: Charles McVicker
Client: United States Air Force

82 Institutional
Artist: **Fred Otnes**
Art Director: Vince Maiello
Client: The Literary Guild

87 Book
Artist: **Ian Miller**
Art Director: Leonard Leone
Title: The Martian Chronicles
Publisher: Bantam Books

84 Institutional
Artist: **Mary Ann Sullivan**
Art Director: Mary Ann Sullivan

85 Advertising
Artist: **Guy Billout**
Art Director: Susan Senk
Client: Lifesong Records

86 Book
Artist: **Edward Soyka**
Art Director: Milton Charles
Title: On All the Seas With Oysters
Publisher: Pocket Books

88 Editorial
Artist: **Gervasio Gallardo**
Art Director: Neil Shakery
Publication: Psychology Today

89 Advertising
Artist: **Al Pisano**
Art Director: Jurgen Kleinfeld
Agency: Lintas: Hamburg, W. Germany
Client: Unilever Corp.

91 Advertising
Artist: **Seymour Chwast**
Art Director: Abie Sussman/Bob Defrin
Client: Atlantic Records

90 Advertising
Artist: **Hodges Soileau**
Art Director: Dick Baker
Agency: Ketchum, McLeod & Grove, Inc.
Client: Kirby Building Systems

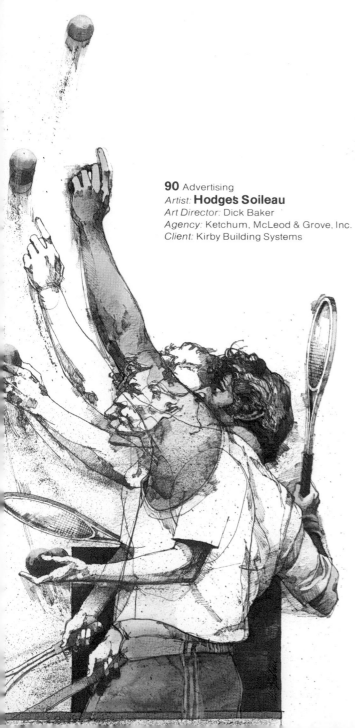

93 Advertising
Artist: **John Schreck**
Art Director: Ron Ketchum
Agency: Ron Ketchum Associates, Inc.
Client: Genesee Brewing Co.

92 Advertising
Artist: **David Willardson**
Art Director: Janet Monte
Agency: Young & Rubicam, Inc.
Client: Chiquita Banana Co.

95 Advertising
Artist: **Harry George**
Art Director: Dave Hartzell
Agency: Carr Liggett Inc.
Client: Ridge Tool

96 Institutional
Artist: **Lynn Gohman**
Art Director: Ed Shorts
Client: Gibson Greeting Cards, Inc.

94 Institutional
Artist: **Frank Loveless**
Art Director: Frank Loveless
Client: Snazzy Art

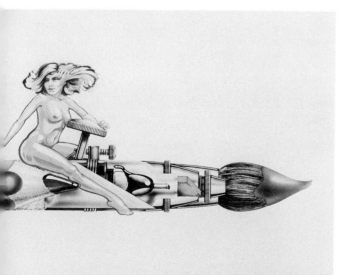

98 Book
Artist: **Walter Spitzmiller**
Art Director: Barbara Bertoli
Title: Pictures That Storm Inside My Head
Publisher: Avon Books

97 Institutional
Artist: **Fred Otnes**
Art Director: Vince Maiello
Client: The Literary Guild

99 Editorial
Artist: **Allan Mardon**
Art Director: Richard Gangel
Publication: Sports Illustrated

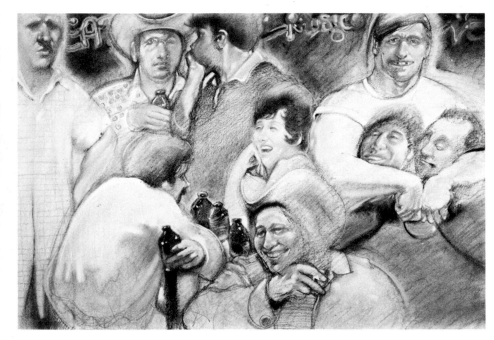

100 Editorial
Artist: **Richard Sparks**
Art Director: Joe Connolly
Publication: Gallery Magazine

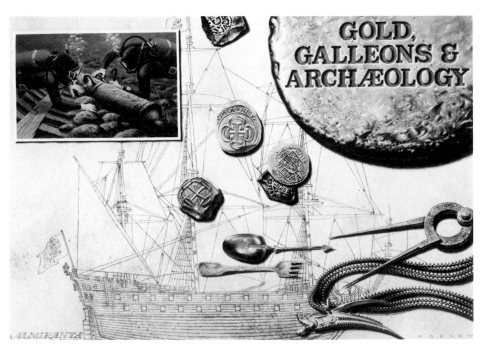

101 Book
Artist: **Howard Koslow**
Art Director: Linda Holiday
Title: Gold Galleons & Archeology
Publisher: Bobbs-Merrill Publishing Co.

102 Book
Artist: **Howard Rogers**
Art Director: William Gregory
Title: Lady in the Lake
Publisher: Reader's Digest

104 Book
Artist: **Ben Wohlberg**
Art Director: William Gregory
Title: Night of the Hunter
Publisher: Reader's Digest

103 Book
Artist: **Jim Sharpe**
Art Director: William Gregory
Title: Rogue Male
Publisher: Reader's Digest

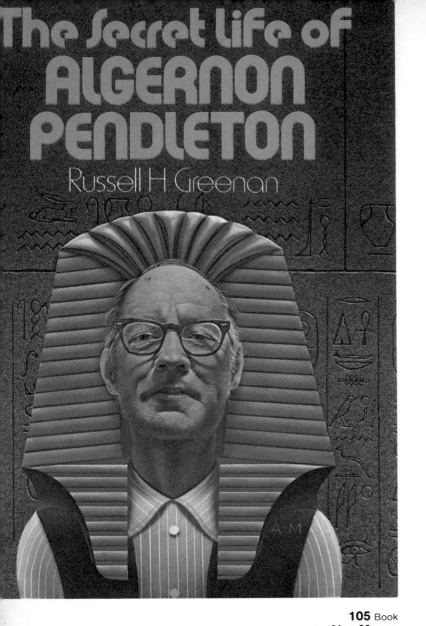

105 Book
Artist: **Alan Magee**
Art Director: Dale Phillips
Title: The Secret Life of Algernon Pendleton
Publisher: Fawcett World Library

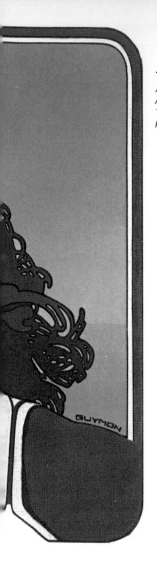

106 Book
Artist: **Linda Fennimore**
Art Director: Rebecca Sacks
Title: A Running Start
Publisher: Quadrangle/The New York Times Book Co.

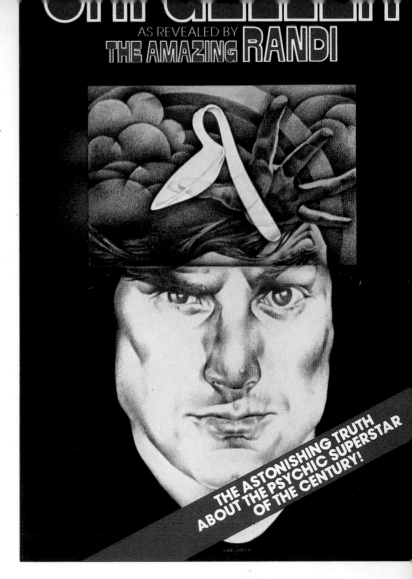

AS REVEALED BY
THE AMAZING RANDI

THE ASTONISHING TRUTH ABOUT THE PSYCHIC SUPERSTAR OF THE CENTURY!

107 Book
Artist: **Richard Waldrep**
Art Director: Ian Summers
Title: The Magic of Uri Geller
Publisher: Ballantine Books, Inc.

108 Institutional
Artist: **Jozef Sumichrast**
Art Director: Lawrence Levy
Client: Society for Visual Education
& New York Botanical Gardens

109 Editorial
Artist: **Renée Faure**
Art Director: Renée Faure
Publication: Jacksonville Magazine

110 Book
Artist: **Barbara Bascove**
Art Director: Harris Lewine
Title: The Nonexistent Knight
Publisher: Harcourt Brace Jovanovich, Inc.

111 Editorial
Artist: **Bart Forbes**
Art Director: Joe Brooks
Publication: Penthouse Magazine

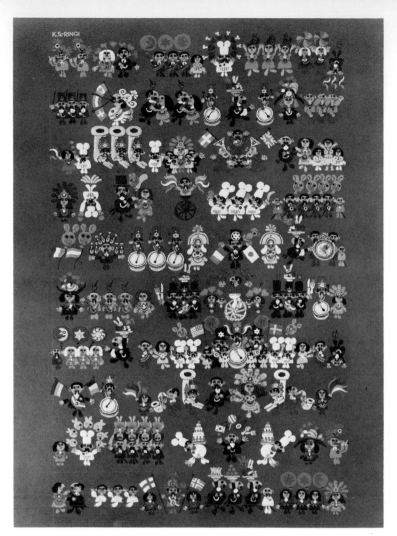

112 Advertising
Artist: **Kjell S. Ringi**
Art Director: Lars-Åke Strömberg
Agency: Kommunikanterna
Client: Park Avenue Hotel
       Gothenburg, Sweden

113 Advertising
Artist: **Greg Speirs**
Art Director: Greg Speirs

IME

ting
he G.O.P

114 Editorial
Artist: **Daniel Schwartz**
Art Director: David Merrill
Publication: Time Magazine

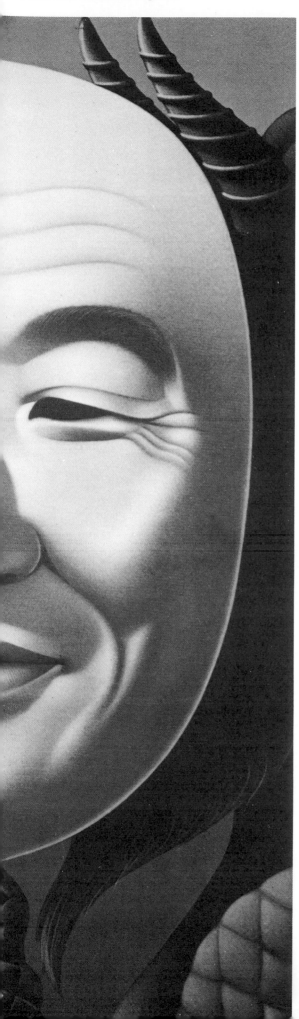

115 Editorial
Artist: **Robert Giusti**
Art Director: Joe Brooks
Publication: Penthouse Magazine

116 Editorial
Artist: **John Thompson**
Art Director: Jerry Demoney
Publication: Seventeen Magazine

117 Editorial
Artist: **Alex Gnidziejko**
Art Director: Alvin Grossman/Modesto Torré
Publication: McCall's Magazine

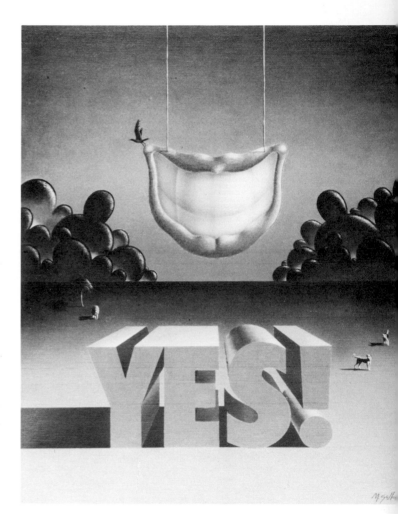

118 Advertising
Artist: **Melinda Bordelon**
Art Director: Stuart Bran
Agency: David, Oksner & Mitchneck
Client: Consolidated Cigar Corp.

120 Institutional
Artist: **Martin Geller**
Art Director: Martin Geller

119 Book
Artist: **Robert Heindel**
Art Director: William Gregory
Title: Psycho
Publisher: Reader's Digest

122 Institutional
Artist: **Daniel Schwartz**
Art Director: Jack Summerford
Agency: The Richards Group
Client: Lomas & Nettleton

21 Editorial
Artist: **Harvey Dinnerstein**
Art Director: Walter Bernard/Milton Glaser
Publication: New York Magazine
ward for Excellence

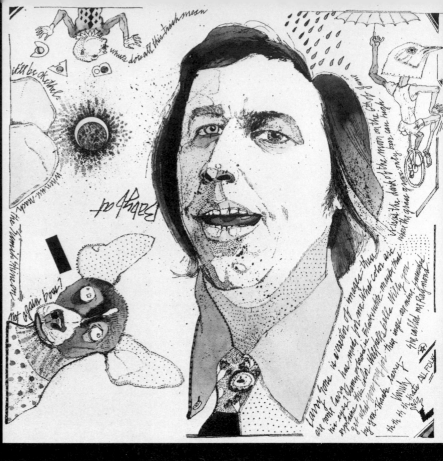

125 Editorial
Artist: **Richard Corson**
Art Director: William A. Motta
Publication: Road & Track

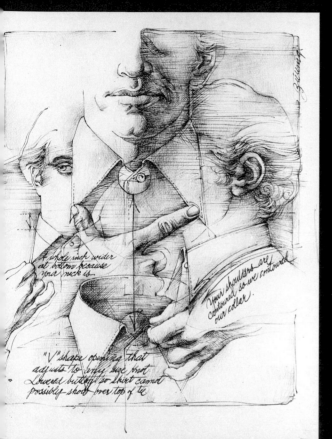

126 Advertising
Artist: **Bob Ziering**
Art Director: Frank DeVito
Agency: Young & Rubicam, Inc.
Client: Arrow Shirts

127 Advertising
Artist: **Cyril David**
Art Director: Cyril David

129 Editorial
Artist: **Dennis Luzak**
Art Director: Don Adamec
Publication: Ladies' Home Journal

128 Advertising
Artist: **David Palladini**
Art Director: Alan Davis
Client: London Records

130 Book
Artist: **Fred Pfeiffer**
Art Director: Leonard Leone
Title: American Review #24
Publisher: Bantam Books

131 Editorial
Artist: **Joe Isom**
Art Director: Jim Leftwich
Publication: Wee Wisdom Magazine

132 Book
Artist: **Chet Jezierski**
Art Director: Leonard Leone
Title: House on Garabaldi Street
Publisher: Bantam Books

133 Editorial
Artist: **Ned Seidler**
Art Director: Howard E. Paine
Publication: National Geographic Magazine

134 Editorial
Artist: **Doug Johnson**
Art Director: Richard Gangel
Publication: Sports Illustrated

135 Television
Artist: **Martin Geller**
Art Director: Beverly Littlewood
Client: WNBC-TV News Center 4

136 Editorial
Artist: **Bart Forbes**
Art Director: Barbara Chapman
Publication: Seventeen Magazine

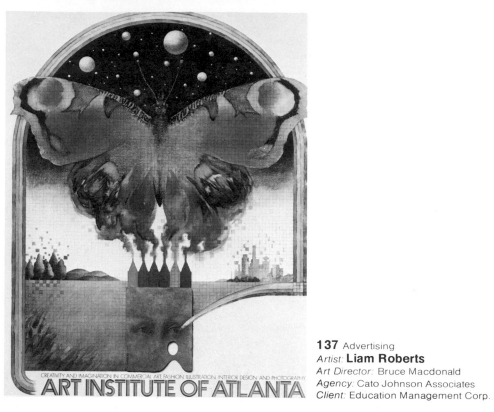

ART INSTITUTE OF ATLANTA

137 Advertising
Artist: **Liam Roberts**
Art Director: Bruce Macdonald
Agency: Cato Johnson Associates
Client: Education Management Corp.

138 Institutional
Artist: **Deanna Glad**
Art Director: Keith Bright
Agency: Keith Bright & Associates
Client: Graphic Process Co.

139 Editorial
Artist: **Louis S. Glanzman**
Art Director: Howard E. Paine
Publication: National Geographic Magazine

140 Book
Artist: **Ann Toulmin-Rothe**
Art Director: Ann Toulmin-Rothe

142 Editorial
Artist: **James McMullan**
Art Director: Richard Gangel
Publication: Sports Illustrated

141 Editorial
Artist: **Tony Eubanks**
Art Director: Tony Eubanks

143 Advertising
Artist: **Allan Mardon**
Art Director: Bob Paige/Dick Loomis
Agency: Evans, Garber, Ligas & Paige
Client: Mohawk Paper Mills, Inc.

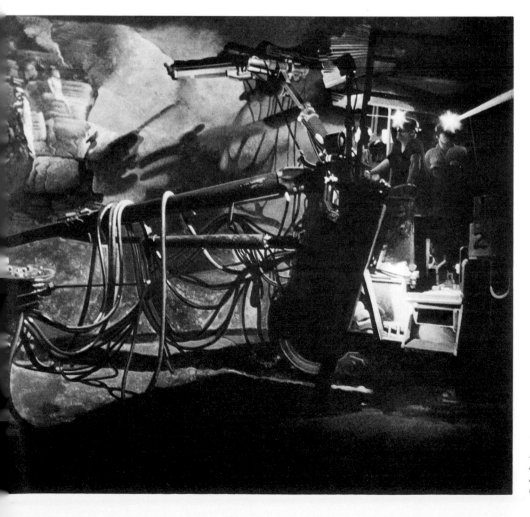

144 Institutional
Artist: **Wilson McLean**
Art Director: Len Fury
Agency: Corporate Annual Reports, Inc.
Client: St. Joe Minerals Corp.

145 Book
Artist: **Jean-Leon Huens**
Art Director: M. Miller/K. P. Sneider
Title: Discovery—Marco Polo
Publisher: Reader's Digest Condensed Books

147 Institutional
Artist: **Walt Spitzmiller**
Art Director: Walt Spitzmiller
Client: Keeler/Morris

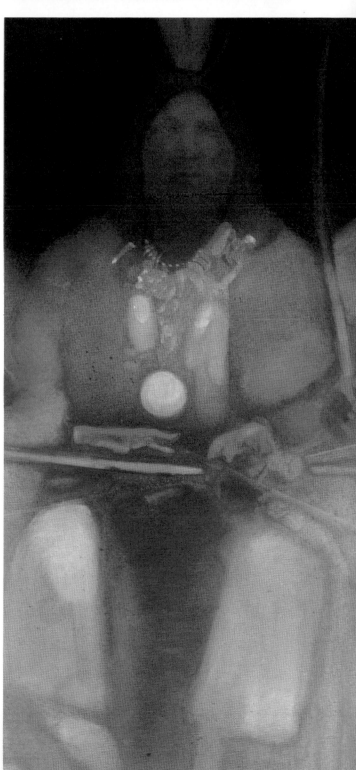

146 Book
Artist: **Jean-Leon Huens**
Art Director: M. Miller/K. P. Sneider
Title: Discovery-Columbus
Publisher: Reader's Digest Condensed Books

148 Institutional
Artist: **Mike Foley**
Art Director: Mike Foley
Agency: Maritz Motivation
Client: Maritz Motivation

149 Editorial
Artist: **Alex Gnidziejko**
Art Director: Alvin Grossman/Modesto Torré
Publication: McCall's Magazine

150 Advertising
Artist: **Brooke Hunyady**
Art Director: Brooke Hunyady

151 Institutional
Artist: **Rainer Koenig**
Art Director: Rainer Koenig

152 Advertising
Artist: **Paul Davis**
Art Director: Marvin Mitchneck
Agency: David, Oksner & Mitchneck
Client: Consolidated Cigar Corp.

154 Editorial
Artist: **Robert Andrew Parker**
Art Director: Adrian Taylor
Publication: Travel & Leisure Magazine

155 Book
Artist: **Erik Sundgaard**
Art Director: Erik Sundgaard

156 Advertising
Artist: **Rudy Lazlo**
Art Director: Paul Maurer
Agency: Ogilvy & Mather, Inc.
Client: The New York Committee for Public
Interest

"Afraid," snorted his father until his n
burned. "A monster of mine afraid? Wha
you afraid of?"

"People," said Clyde. "I'm afraid there
people in there who will get me."

157 Institutional
Artist: **Linda E. Gist**
Art Director: Linda E. Gist

158 Advertising
Artist: **Gary Overacre**
Art Director: David Bartels
Agency: Clinton & Frank, Inc.
Client: Dean's Foods

159 Book
Artist: **Kay Chorao**
Art Director: Riki Levinson
Title: Clyde Monster
Publisher: E. P. Dutton & Co., inc.

160 Book
Artist: **Frank Frazetta**
Art Director: Gene Light
Title: Dark Crusade
Publisher: Warner Books

161 Advertising
Artist: **Wilson McLean**
Art Director: John Berg
Client: CBS Records

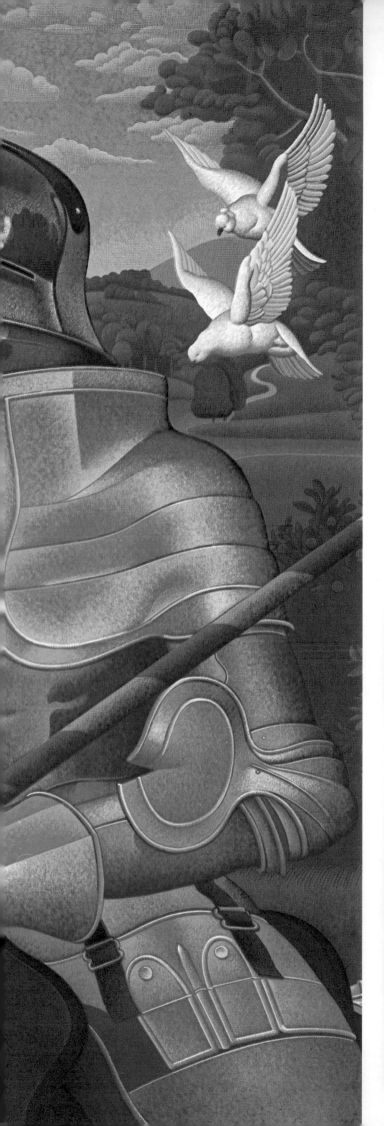

162 Book
Artist: Steve Karchin
Art Director: Barbara Bertoli
Title: Morning Watch
Publisher: Avon Books

163 Book
Artist: **Richard Krepel**
Art Director: Stan Friedman
Title: Re-Enter Fu Manchu
Publisher: Pyramid Publications

165 Editorial
Artist: **Allan Mardon**
Art Director: Richard Gangel
Publication: Sports Illustrated

164 Advertising
Artist: **Robert Schulz**
Art Director: Horalto Alvis
Agency: Tinker, Campbell, Ewald
Client: Heublein, Inc.

166 Editorial
Artist: **Jamie Putnam**
Art Director: Tony Lane
Publication: Rolling Stone

167 Institutional
Artist: **Jerry Karl**
Art Director: Jerry Karl

168 Editorial
Artist: **Dennis Smith**
Art Director: Richard D. Brown
Publication: The Friend Magazine

169 Institutional
Artist: **George H. Rothacker**
Art Director: George H. Rothacker
Client: A. V. Wood Marketing Services

170 Advertising
Artist: **Richard K. Miller**
Art Director: Richard K. Miller

171 Advertising
Artist: **Roy Andersen**
Art Director: Jim Hedden
Agency: Bill Gold Advertising, Inc.
Client: Avco Embassy

172 Advertising
Artist: **Philip J. Marshall, Jr.**
Art Director: Elizabeth Leibman
Agency: Hefferan, Hastie & Leibman

173 Advertising
Artist: **David Levine**
Art Director: Henrietta Condak/John Berg
Client: CBS Records

174 Advertising
Artist: **Doug Johnson**
Art Director: Ed Leahy
Agency: Batten, Barton, Durstine & Osborn, Inc.

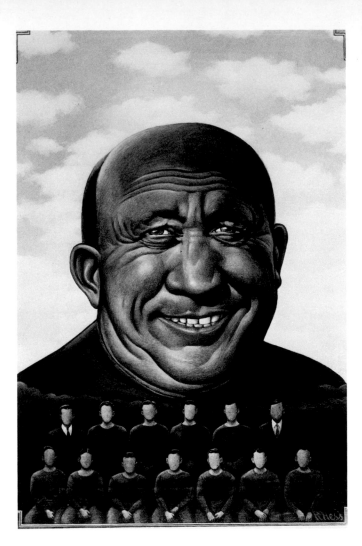

175 Book
Artist: **Richard Hess**
Art Director: Paul Gamarello
Title: Rockne
Publisher: Random House, Inc.
Award for Excellence

176 Institutional
Artist: **Etienne Delessert**
Art Director: Etienne Delessert
Client: Musée des Arts Décoratifs

178 Book
Artist: **Richard Krepel**
Art Director: Stan Friedman
Title: The Island of Fu Manchu
Publisher: Pyramid Publications

177 Advertising
Artist: **John Dyess**
Art Director: Curt Simpson
Agency: Maritz Motivation
Client: Exide

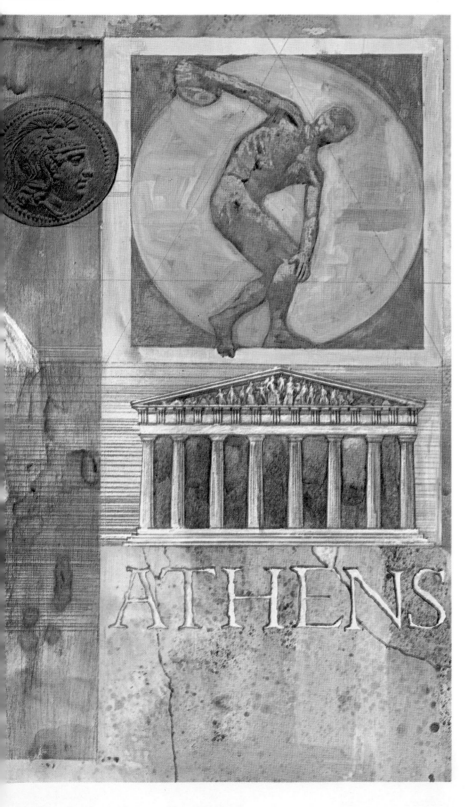

179 Book
Artist: **Richard Krepel**
Art Director: Stan Friedman
Title: The Drums of Fu Manchu
Publisher: Pyramid Publications

182 Editorial
Artist: **Tony Eubanks**
Art Director: Tony Eubanks

180 Advertising
Artist: **Ed Acuña**
Art Director: Murlin Marsh
Client: NBC Television

181 Editorial
Artist: **Dick Lubey**
Art Director: Dick Luby

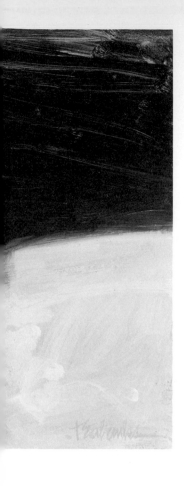

183 Advertising
Artist: **Frances Melendez**
Art Director: Charles Lilly

184 Advertising
Artist: **Richard F. Newton**
Art Director: Richard F. Newton

186 Book
Artist: **David Passalacqua**
Art Director: Leonard Leone
Title: Stigmata of Dr. Constantine
Publisher: Bantam Books

187 Book
Artist: **Vin Giuliani**
Art Director: John Van Zwienen
Title: The Future of Being Human
Publisher: Dell Publishing Co.

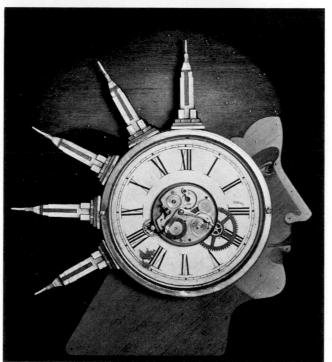

188 Book
Artist: **Alan Magee**
Art Director: Ian Summers
Title: We Almost Lost Detroit
Publisher: Ballantine Books, Inc.

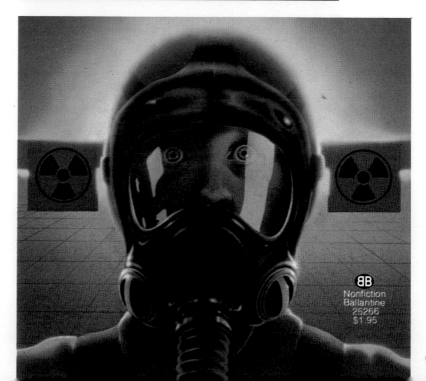

185 Editorial
Artist: **David Wilcox**
Art Director: Joe Brooks
Publication: Penthouse Magazine

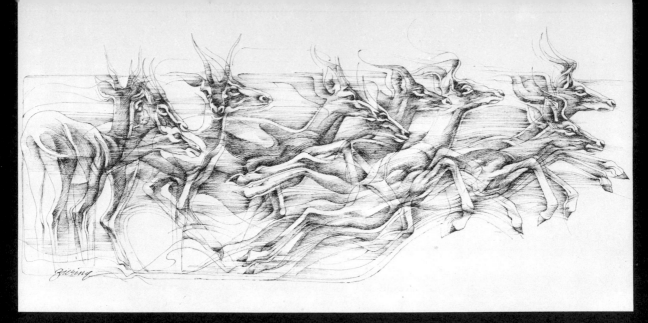

189 Advertising
Artist: **Bob Ziering**
Art Director: Howard Kates
Agency: N. W. Ayer ABH International
Client: T.V. Guide

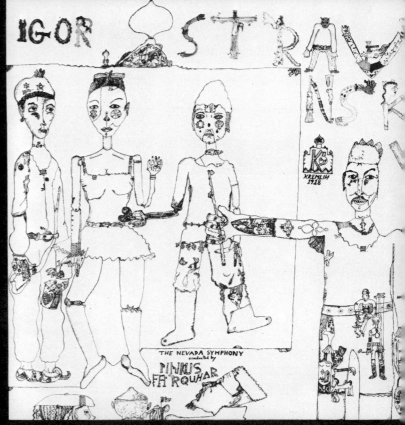

190 Advertising
Artist: **Joseph Pomerance**
Art Director: Joseph Pomerance

191 Institutional
Artist: **Gary Kelley**
Art Director: Gary Kelley
Client: Hellman Design Associates, Inc.

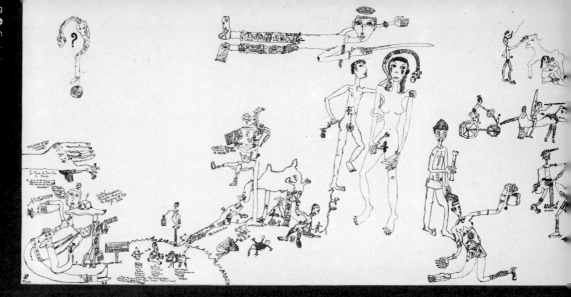

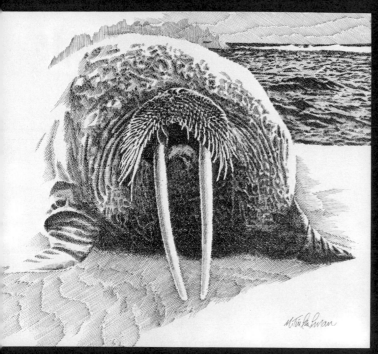

116 Book
Artist: **Ted CoConis**
Art Director: Vincent Perry
Title: Kit Carson
Publisher: Reader's Digest

197 Editorial
Artist: **Herb Tauss**
Art Director:
Sal Lazzarotti/Jessica Weber
Publication: Guideposts Magazine

198 Editorial
Artist: **Ivan Paslavsky**
Art Director: Ivan Paslavsky

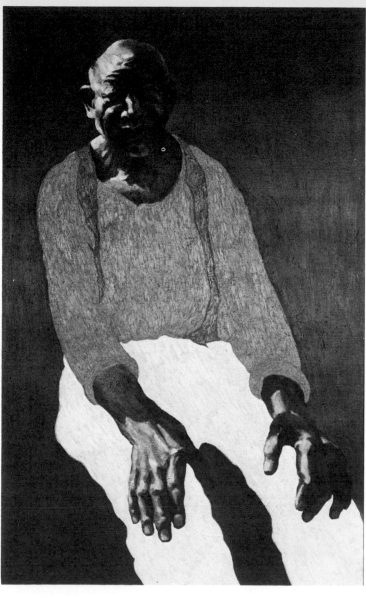

201 Editorial
Artist: **Richard Farrell**
Art Director: Richard Farrell

202 Editorial
Artist: **G. Hyer**
Art Director: G. Hyer

00 Editorial
tist: **Maurice Lewis**
t Director: Don Willis
blication: Shell Chemical Co.

204 Editorial
Artist: **Mark English**
Art Director: William Cadge
Publication: Redbook Magazine
Gold Medal

203 Book
Artist: **Charles Gehm**
Art Director: Barbara Bertoli
Title: All God's Dangers
Publisher: Avon Books

205 Advertising
Artist: **Lance R. Miyamoto**
Art Director: Lance R. Miyamoto

206 Editorial
Artist: **Edward Sorel**
Art Director: William Cadge
Publication: Redbook Magazine

207 Institutional
Artist: **Fred Otnes**
Art Director: Harry O. Diamond
Client: Exxon Corp.

208 Editorial
Artist: **Brad Holland**
Art Director: Arthur Paul/Robert Post
Publication: Playboy

209 Institutional
Artist: **James McMullan**
Art Director: Carol Carson
Client: Scholastic Magazine

210 Editorial
Artist: **James C. Christensen**
Art Director: James C. Christensen
Publication: New Era Magazine

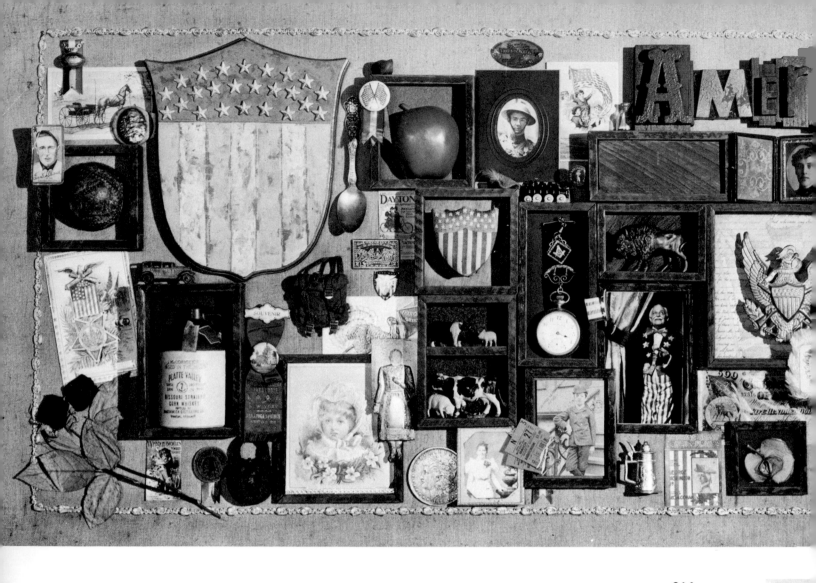

214 Advertising
Artist: **Ted CoConis**
Art Director: Ace Lehman
Client: RCA Records

212 Book
Artist: **Jack Hayes**
Art Director: Leonard Leone
Title: Angelique in Barbary
Publisher: Bantam Books

213 Book
Artist: **Steve Karchin**
Art Director: Barbara Bertoli
Title: The Awakened
Publisher: Avon Books

211 Advertising
Artist: **Gerald McConnell**
Art Director: Joseph Stelmach
Client: RCA Records

217 Institutional
Artist: **Robert Schulz**
Art Director: Robert Schulz

218 Institutional
Artist: **Bob Peak**
Art Director: Bob Peak
Client: Jack O'Grady Galleries, Inc.

219 Editorial
Artist: **Noel Sickles**
Art Director: Howard E. Paine
Publication: National Geographic Magazine

220 Advertising
Artist: **Mark English**
Art Director: Jack O'Grady
Client: Jack O'Grady Galleries, Inc.

221 Advertising
Artist: **Heather Cooper**
Art Director: Heather Cooper

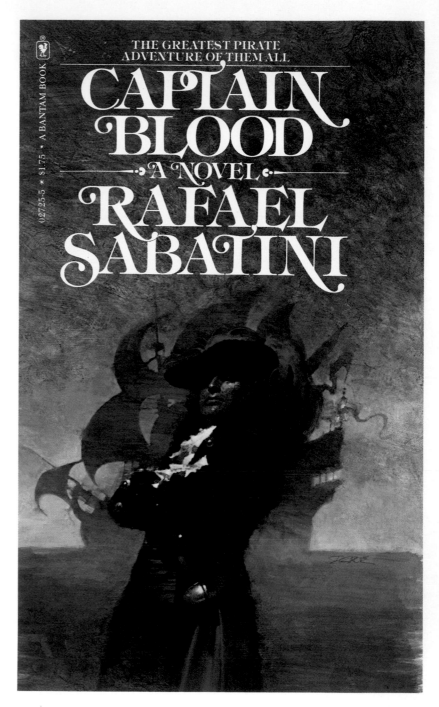

THE GREATEST PIRATE
ADVENTURE OF THEM ALL

CAPTAIN
BLOOD
A NOVEL
RAFAEL
SABATINI

222 Editorial
Artist: **Alan E. Cober**
Art Director: Neil Shakery
Publication: Psychology Today

223 Book
Artist: **David Grove**
Art Director: Leonard Leone
Title: Captain Blood
Publisher: Bantam Books

224 Editorial
Artist: **Ed Lindlof**
Art Director: Ed Lindlof
Publication: Texas Parade Magazine

225 Editorial
Artist: **Daniel Schwartz**
Art Director: Ronald Campbell
Publication: Fortune Magazine

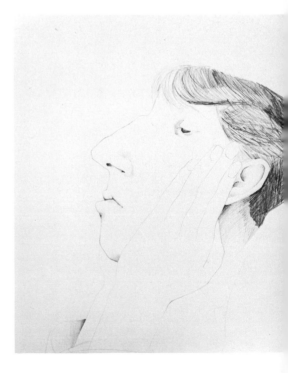

227 Editorial
Artist: **Judith Jampel**
Art Director: Joe Brooks
Publication: Penthouse Magazine

228 Editorial
Artist: **John Robinette**
Art Director: Jack Atkinson/Fred Woodward
Publication: City of Memphis Magazine

226 Book
Artist: **Jill Bossert**
Art Director: Jill Bossert

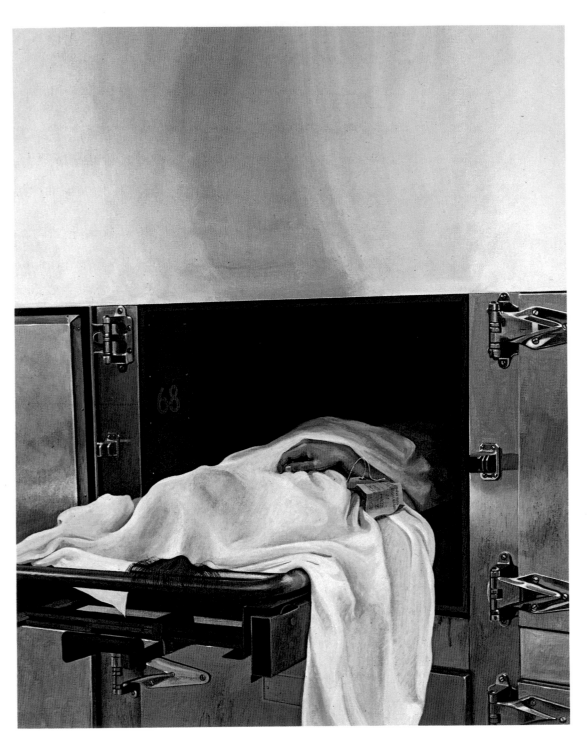

229 Book
Artist: **Wendell Minor**
Art Director: Frank Metz
Title: City of the Dead
Publisher: Simon & Schuster, Inc.

230 Book
Artist: **Robert McGinnis**
Art Director: Barbara Bertoli
Title: The Land Remembers
Publisher: Avon Books

231 Advertising
Artist: **Bruce Wolfe**
Art Director: Chris Blum
Agency: Foote, Cone/Honig
Client: Levi-Strauss International

232 Institutional
Artist: **Tim & Greg Hildebrandt**
Art Director: Ian Summers
Client: Ballantine Books, Inc.

233 Book
Artist: **Jared D. Lee**
Art Director: Edythe Draper
Title: Care and Feeding
Publisher: Tyndale House

234 Institutional
Artist: **Bernie Karlin**
Art Director: Al Catalano
Agency: AKM Associates Inc.
Client: American Telephone & Telegraph

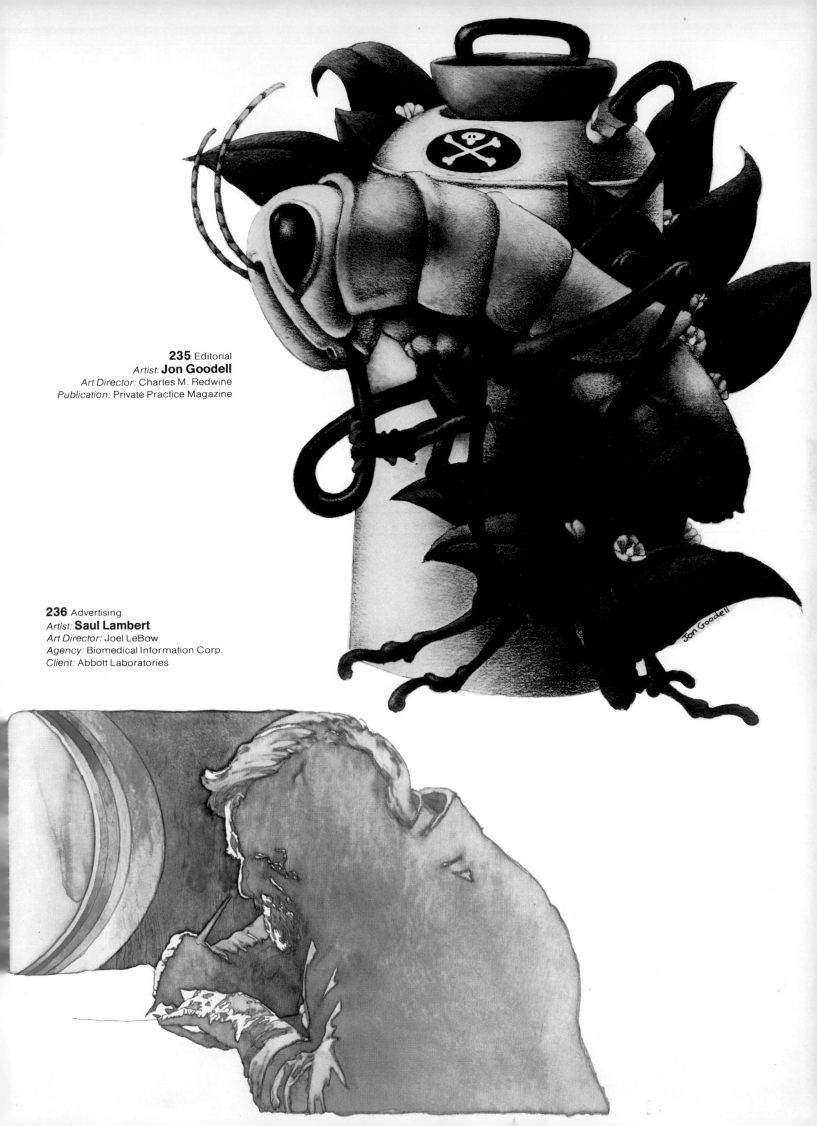

235 Editorial
Artist: **Jon Goodell**
Art Director: Charles M. Redwine
Publication: Private Practice Magazine

236 Advertising
Artist: **Saul Lambert**
Art Director: Joel LeBow
Agency: Biomedical Information Corp.
Client: Abbott Laboratories

237 Book
Artist: **John Thompson**
Art Director: Skip Sorvino
Title: Liquid Trap
Publisher: Scholastic Book Services

238 Advertising
Artist: **Carlos Ochagavia**
Art Director: Al Zakin
Agency: Zakin & Comerford
Client: Broadcast Music Inc.

240 Editorial
Artist: **Bob Dacey**
Art Director: Joe Connolly
Publication: Gallery Magazine

239 Advertising
Artist: **Bruce Wolfe**
Art Director: David Bartels
Agency: Clinton E. Frank Co.
Client: Dean's Foods

241 Book
Artist: **Bernard P. Colonna**
Art Director: Dann Jacobus
Title: A Pack of Dreams
Publisher: Prentice-Hall, Inc.

242 Book
Artist: **Don Ivan Punchatz**
Art Director: Gene Light
Title: Giant Rat of Sumatra
Publisher: Warner Books

243 Book
Artist: **Dave Christensen**
Art Director: Alex Gotfryd
Title: Now and Another Time
Publisher: Doubleday & Co., Inc.

244 Advertising
Artist: **James Reynolds**
Art Director: Ria Lewerke
Client: United Artists Records

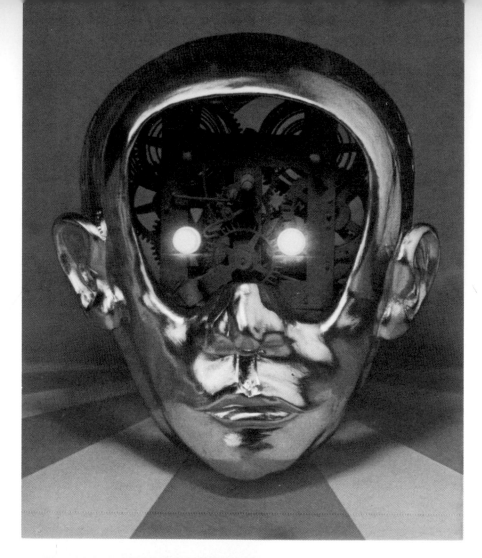

245 Book
Artist: **Marilyn Bass/Marvin Goldm**
Art Director: Marilyn Bass/Marvin Goldm
Publisher: Reader's Digest

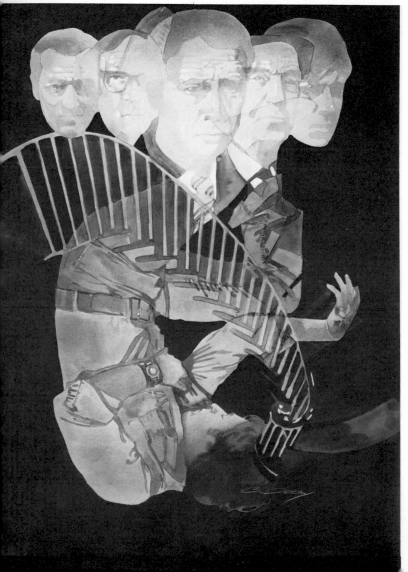

247 Advertising
Artist: **Bob Dacey**
Art Director: Bob Dacey
Client: Mulvey Associates

246 Institutional
Artist: **Bob Dacey**
Art Director: Tom Reis
Publication: American Way

248 Institutional
Artist: **Roy Andersen**
Art Director: Louann Ihde

249 Advertising
Artist: **Roy Andersen**
Art Director: Bill Gold
Agency: Bill Gold Advertising, Inc.
Client: Warner Bros.

250 Editorial
Artist: **Bob Peak**
Art Director: David Merrill
Publication: Time Magazine

Messengers
of Love and Hope
LIVING
SAINTS

251 Advertising
Artist: **Edward Sorel**
Art Director: John Berg
Client: CBS Records

252 Book
Artist: **Robert Katona**
Art Director: Betty Anderson
Title: Golden Eagle Country
Publisher: Alfred A. Knopf

253 Advertising
Artist: **Jim Endicott**
Art Director: Talbart Smith
Agency: Wenger-Michael Inc.
Client: Fender Musical Instruments

254 Advertising
Artist: **Bart Forbes**
Art Director: Hillen Smith
Client: USF&G Insurance Co.

256 Editorial
Artist: **Richard Sparks**
Art Director: Joseph Connolly
Publication: Boys' Life Magazine

255 Editorial
Artist: **Bob Kuhn**
Art Director: Victor J. Closi
Publication: Field & Stream Magazine

257 Advertis
Artist: **Jerry Pinkn**
Art Director: Ralph Moxcey/Jim Witha
Agency: Humphrey, Browning, MacDou
Client: S. D. Warren Paper C

As I was going to St. Ives,
I met a man with seven wives.
Each wife had seven sacks,
Each sack had seven cats,
Each cat had seven kits,
Kits, cats, sacks, and wives,
How many were there going to St. Ives?

40

258 Editorial
Artist: **Brad Holland**
Art Director: Steve Heller
Publication: The New York Times

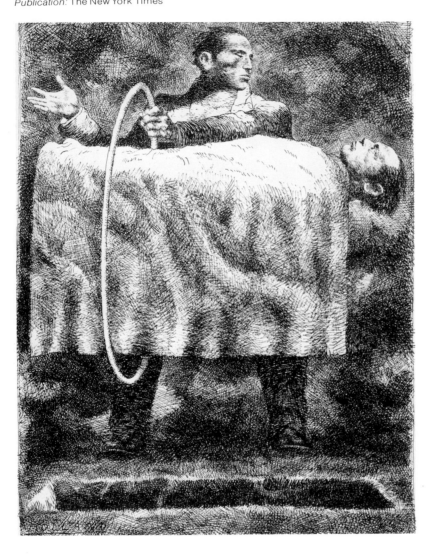

260 Book
Artist: **Alice & Martin Provensen**
Art Director: Grace Clarke
Title: The Mother Goose Book
Publisher: Random House, Inc.

259 Advertising
Artist: **Heather Cooper**
Art Director: Robert Burns
Agency: Burns, Cooper, Donoahue, Fleming
& Co., Ltd.
Client: Abitibi Provincial Paper Co.

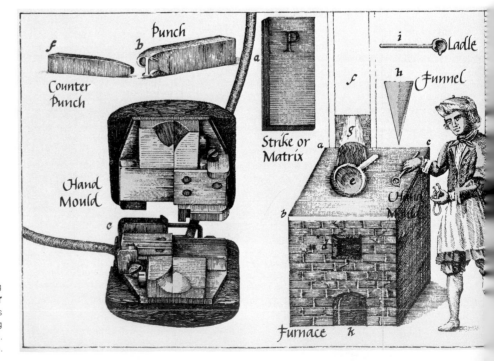

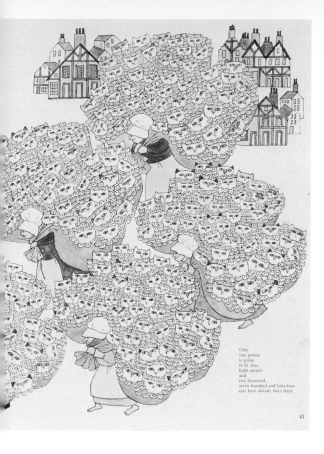

Only
one person
is going
to St. Ives.
Eight people
and
two thousand,
seven hundred and forty-four
cats have already been there

41

261 Book
Artist: **William Murphy**
Art Director: Bob Feldgus
Title: Auto Album 2
Publisher: Scholastic Book Services

262 Advertising
Artist: **Cliff Condak**
Art Director: Cliff Condak/Henrietta Condak
Agency: C & H Condak
Client: Rodale Press

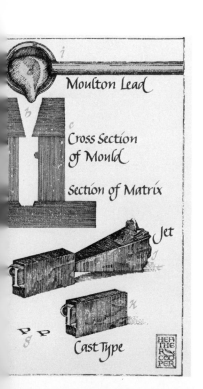

263 Editorial
Artist: **Craig Nelson**
Art Director: Art Aveilhe
Publication: Players Magazine

264 Advertising
Artist: **Greg King**
Art Director: Woody Pirtle
Agency: The Richards Group
Client: TM Productions, Inc.

265 Book
Artist: **Roy Andersen**
Art Director: Ian Summers
Title: Moe Berg Athlete, Scholar…Spy
Publisher: Ballantine Books, Inc.

266 Advertising
Artist: **Joanne Scribner**
Art Director: Leonard Restivo/Nancy Bradley
Client: Bloomingdale's

267 Editorial
Artist: **Gilbert Stone**
Art Director: Joe Brooks
Publication: Penthouse Magazine

268 Editorial
Artist: **Elizabeth Bennett**
Art Director: Arthur Paul
Publication: Playboy

269 Editorial
Artist: **Elizabeth Bennett**
Art Director: Arthur Paul
Publication: Playboy

270 Institutional
Artist: **Paul Giovanopoulos**
Art Director: Paul Giovanopoulos

271 Institutional
Artist: **Charles Schorre**
Art Director: Charles Schorre
Client: DuBose Gallery

273 Bo
Artist: **David Grov**
Art Director: Leonard Leo
Title: Coffin Full of Drear
Publisher: Bantam Boc

272 Book
Artist: **Wendell Minor**
Art Director: Louise Noble
Title: The Year The Lights Came On
Publisher: Houghton Mifflin Co.

274 Advertising
Artist: **Dave Jarvis**
Art Director: Ace Lehman
Client: RCA Records

275 Institutional
Artist: **Hodges Soileau**
Art Director: Hodges Soileau

276 Institutional
Artist: **Eugene Karlin**
Art Director: Ken Jordan
Client: Geigy Pharmaceuticals

277 Institutional
Artist: **Lee Bonner**
Art Director: Joe Caserta
Client: Consolidated Drake

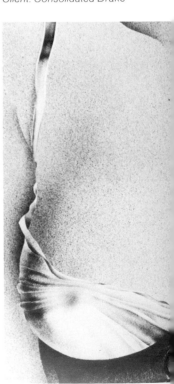

278 Book
Artist: **Sanford Kossin**
Art Director: Leonard Leone
Title: Is There Sex After Death
Publisher: Bantam Books

279 Institutional
Artist: **Carole Jean**
Art Director: Carole Jean

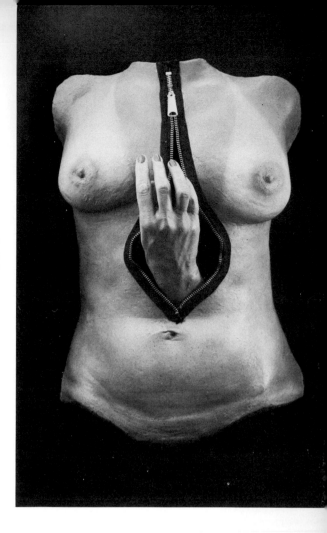

280 Editorial
Artist: **Larry A. Gerber**
Art Director: Seymour Gerber
Agency: G/D Advertising, Inc.
Client: Braniff International

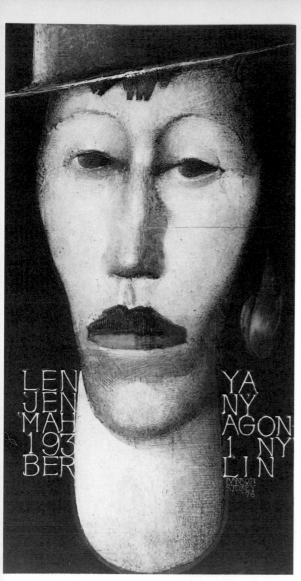

281 Advertising
Artist: **Barron Storey**
Art Director: Robert Paige/Richard Loomis
Agency: Evans, Ligas & Paige
Client: Mohawk Paper Mills, Inc.
Gold Medal

282 Editorial
Artist: **Mel Odom**
Art Director: Rowan Johnson
Publication: Viva Magazine

283 Advertising
Artist: **Charles B. Slackman**
Art Director: Rod Capawana
Agency: Doremus & Co.
Client: Bank of New York

285 Advertising
Artist: **Eugene Karlin**
Art Director: David Seabert
Client: CIBA-Geigy Corp.

284 Editorial
Artist: **Murray Tinkelman**
Art Director: Murray Tinkelman

286 Book
Artist: **Herb Steinberg**
Art Director: Diana Klemin
Title: Rebels and Reformers
Publisher: Doubleday & Co., Inc.

288 Advertising
Artist: **Joseph Pomerance**
Art Director: Joseph Pomerance

289 Advertising
Artist: **Dennis Pohl**
Art Director: Bob Heimall
Client: Arista Records

290 Advertising
Artist: **Burt Silverman**
Art Director: Edwin Lee
Client: CBS Records

291 Advertising
Artist: **Alan Reingold**
Art Director: Dick Smith
Client: RCA Records

292 Advertising
Artist: **Miriam Brofsky**
Art Director: Joseph Stelmach
Client: RCA Records

293 Institutional
Artist: **Bart Forbes**
Art Director: Greg Wilder
Agency: Sun Graphics

294 Editorial
Artist: **Norm Walker**
Art Director: Joseph Mauro
Publication: Gallery Magazine

295 Book
Artist: **Jim Sharpe**
Art Director: William Gregory
Title: Rogue Male
Publisher: Reader's Digest

298 Institutional
Artist: **Allan Mardon**
Art Director: Allan Mardon

297 Book
Artist: **Miriam Slater**
Art Director: Miriam Slater

296 Editorial
Artist: **John Collier**
Art Director: Modesto Torré
Publication: McCall's Magazine

299 Institutional
Artist: **Jerry Pinkney**
Art Director: Al Mohr
Agency: Frederick Siebel Associates
Client: Seagrams

300 Book
Artist: **Leo & Diane Dillon**
Art Director: Atha Tehon
Title: Ashanti to Zulu: African Traditions
Publisher: The Dial Press

301 Book
Artist: **Jack Endewelt**
Art Director: Vincent Perry
Title: Fountain of Youth
Publisher: Reader's Digest

302 Editorial
Artist: **Ted Michener**
Art Director: Peter Sypnowich
Publication: Toronto Star

Doctors threaten to strike over pay

303 Book
Artist: **Murray Tinkelman**
Art Director: Ian Summers
Title: The Sheep Look Up
Publisher: Ballantine Books, Inc.

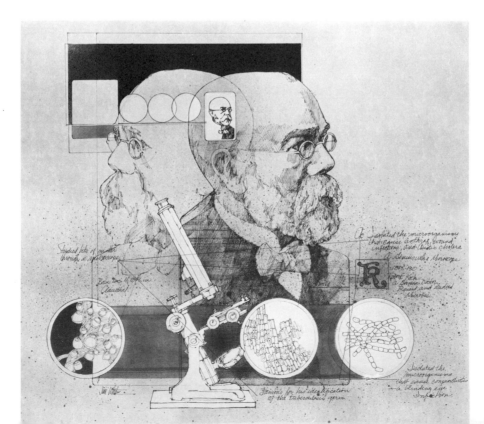

304 Advertising
Artist: **Jim White**
Art Director: Jim White
Client: Stephens-Biondi-DeCicco

305 Book
Artist: **Sanford Kossin**
Art Director: Leonard Leone
Title: Is There Sex After Death
Publisher: Bantam Books

306 Book
Artist: **James Grashow**
Art Director: Lidia Ferrara
Title: Doctor Rat
Publisher: Alfred A. Knopf

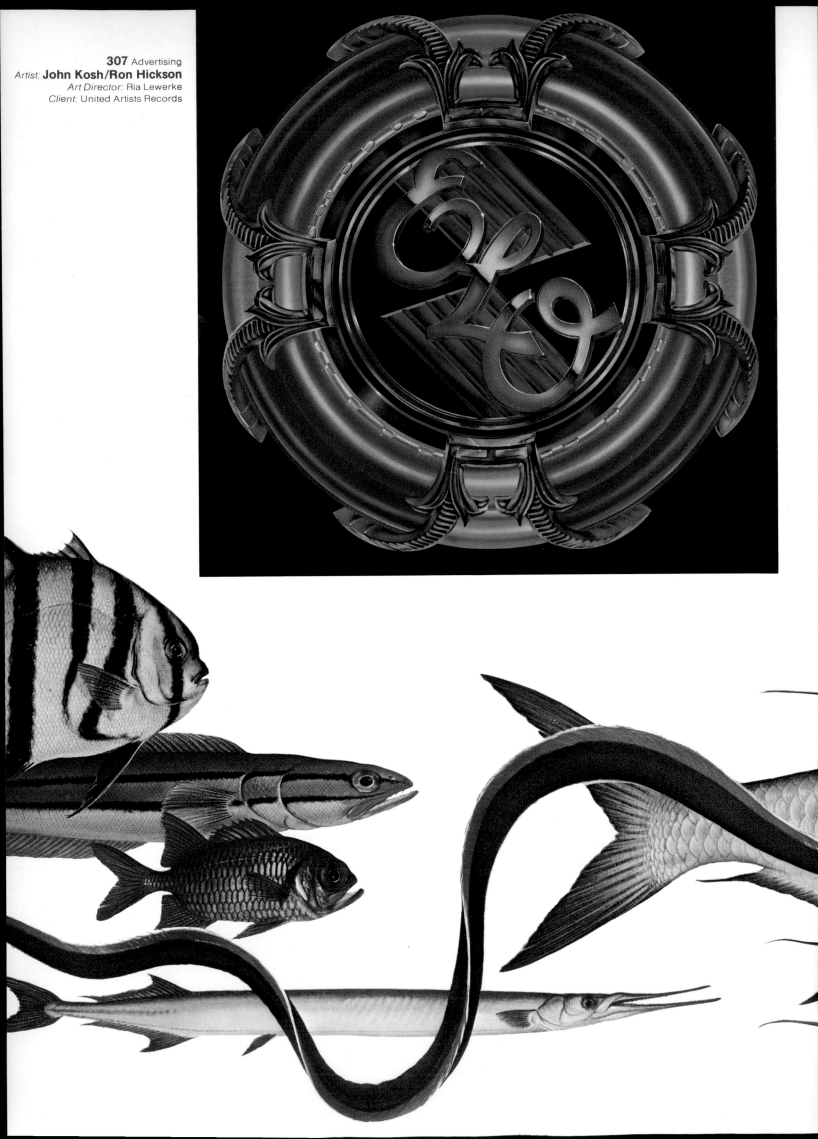

308 Book
Artist: **Chet Jezierski**
Art Director: Robert D. Reed
Title: The Conquerors
Publisher: Holt, Rinehart & Winston, Inc.

309 Book
Artist: **Norman Weaver**
Art Director: Joe Troutwein/R. D. Scudellari
Title: Fresh and Salt Water Fishes of the World
Publisher: Vineyard Books/Alfred A. Knopf

313 Book
Artist: **John Sposato**
Art Director: Ann Spinelli
Title: Who is Teddy Villanova
Publisher: Delacorte Press

314 Institutional
Artist: **Gloria Singer**
Art Director: Gloria Singer
Client: Nu-Line Advertising

316 Book
Artist: **Raymond Ameijide**
Art Director: Leonard Leone
Publisher: Bantam Books

317 Editorial
Artist: **Jim Sharpe**
Art Director: Jerry Alten
Publication: T. V. Guide

315 Advertising
Artist: **Carol Anthony**
Art Director: Joseph Stelmach
Client: RCA Records

318 Advertising
Artist: **Fred Otnes**
Art Director: Robert Geissmann
Client: Society of Illustrators

319 Editorial
Artist: **Jim Campbell**
Art Director: Phillip Dykstra/William L. Bloedow
Publication: Geriatrics

320 Editorial
Artist: **Fred Otnes**
Art Director: Bruce Danbrot/Don Adamec
Publication: Ladies' Home Journal

321 Book
Artist: **Dennis Luzak**
Art Director: William Gregory
Title: The Tide of Life
Publisher: Reader's Digest

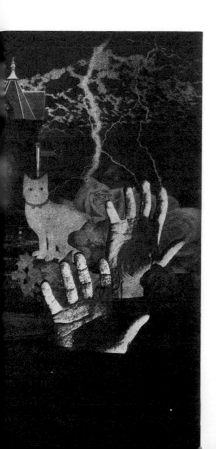

322 Editorial
Artist: **Rick McCollum**
Art Director: Leo McCarthy/Lester Goodman
Publication: Swank Magazine

323 Advertising
Artist: **Mark English**
Art Director: Jack O'Grady
Client: Jack O'Grady Galleries, Inc.

327 Institutional
Artist: **Annie Butte**
Art Director: Bruce Butte
Agency: Bruce and Annie Butte Design
Client: Commercial Printing Co.

325 Advertising
Artist: **Gervasio Gallardo**
Art Director: Gervasio Gallardo

326 Book
Artist: **Gene Szafran**
Art Director: Soren Noring
Title: We Almost Lost Detroit
Publisher: Reader's Digest

328 Institutional
Artist: **Isadore Seltzer**
Art Director: Isadore Seltzer

329 Editorial
Artist: **Eraldo Carugati**
Art Director: Gordon Mortensen
Publication: Skeptic Magazine

330 Institutional

Artist: **Annie Butte**

Art Director: Bruce Butte

Agency: Bruce and Annie Butte Design

Client: Commercial Printing Co.

331 Advertising
Artist: **Arthur Singer**
Art Director: Joseph Stelmach
Client: RCA Records

332 Institutional
Artist: **Mike Robins**
Art Director: Mike Robins
Agency: Mike Robins Studio
Client: Art Directors Club of Houston

333 Advertising
Artist: **Guy Billout**
Art Director: Bob Heimall
Client: Arista Records

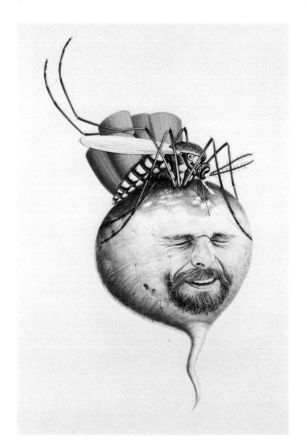

334 Editorial
Artist: **Eraldo Carugati**
Art Director: Arthur Paul
Publication: Playboy

335 Book
Artist: **Joanne L. Scribner**
Art Director: Bruce W. Hall
Title: The Thing at the Foot of the Bed
Publisher: Dell Publishing Co.

336 Book
Artist: **Molly Garrett Bang**
Art Director: Alan Benjamin
Title: Wiley and the Hairy Man
Publisher: Macmillan Publishing Co., Inc.

337 Advertising
Artist: **Gervasio Gallardo**
Art Director: Ed Nussbaum
Agency: Grey Advertising
Client: Greyhound Corp.

338 Book
Artist: **Wayne Anderson**
Art Director: Tom Maschler
Title: Ratsmagic
Publisher: Pantheon Books

339 Book
Artist: **Etienne Delessert**
Art Director: Etienne Delessert
Title: Mouse and Butterflies
Publisher: Riddlehauve Verlag

340 Book
Artist: **Sean Early**
Art Director: Gene Light
Title: The Other Side of Henry Winkler
Publisher: Warner Books

341 Advertising
Artist: **Mark English**
Art Director: Dennis McLaughlin
Client: National Parks Service

342 Advertising
Artist: **Bob Peak**
Art Director: Bob Peak
Client: Jack O'Grady Galleries, Inc.

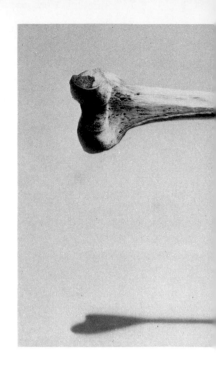

343 Advertising
Artist: **Carol Anthony**
Art Director: Joseph Stelmach
Client: RCA Records

344 Editorial
Artist: **Doug Johnson**
Art Director: Neil Shakery
Publication: Psychology Today

345 Editorial
Artist: **Alan Magee**
Art Director: Joe Brooks
Publication: Penthouse Magazine

346 Editorial
Artist: **Al Pisano**
Art Director: Joe Csatari
Publication: Boy's Life Magazine

347 Book
Artist: **Wayne Anderson**
Art Director: Tom Maschler
Title: Ratsmagic
Publisher: Pantheon Books
Gold Medal

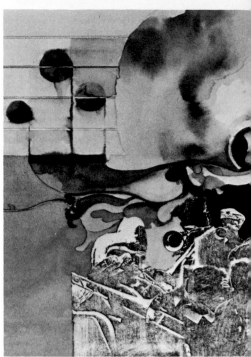

348 Advertising
Artist: **Mike Durbin**
Art Director: Mike Durbin

349 Boo
Artist: **David Passalacqu**
Art Director: Leonard Leo
Title: Memoirs of Hecate Cour
Publisher: Bantam Boo

350 Book
Artist: **Stella Ormai**
Art Director: Carol Mitchell
Title: Moon Mouse
Publisher: Houghton Mifflin Co.

351 Book
Artist: **John Berkey**
Art Director: John Berkey

352 Book
Artist: **Daniel Schwartz**
Art Director: Mike Palombo
Title: Puzzlements, Vol. 2
Publisher: Westvaco

353 Institutional
Artist: **Lemuel Line**
Art Director: Lemuel Line

354 Book
Artist: **Jeffrey Seaver**
Art Director: Jeffrey Seaver

355 Advertising
Artist: **Bernard Fuchs**
Art Director: Jack O'Grady
Client: Jack O'Grady Galleries, Inc.

356 Editorial
Artist: **Bart Forbes**
Art Director: Modesto Torré
Publication: McCall's Magazine

357 Book
Artist: **Barnett Plotkin**
Art Director: Barnett Plotkin

358 Book
Artist: **Walter Rane**
Art Director: Charles Volpe
Title: The Mind Spider
Publisher: Ace Books

359 Book
Artist: **Carlos Antonio Llerena**
Art Director: Miriam Chaikin
Title: Puma Becomes The Otorongo
Publisher: Holt, Rinehart & Winston, Inc.

360 Television
Artist: **Lisberger Studios Inc. (Animation)**
Art Director: Jack Foley
Client: WGBH-TV
Award For Excellence

361 Advertising
Artist: **Alex Ebel**
Art Director: Elmer Pizzi
Agency: Gray & Rogers, Inc.
Client: Grit Magazine

362 Book
Artist: **Lucinda Emily McQueen**
Art Director: Lucinda Emily McQueen

363 Advertising
Artist: **Jerry L. Cosgrove**
Art Director: John Vise
Client: Xerox Corp.

364 Editorial
Artist: **Alan E. Cober**
Art Director: Richard Gangel
Publication: Sports Illustrated

365 Editorial
Artist: **Robert M. Cunningham**
Art Director: David Stech
Publication: Signature Magazine

366 Book
Artist: **John C. Wallner**
Art Director: Barbara Hennessy
Title: Little Fox Goes to the End of the World
Publisher: Crown Publishers, Inc.

367 Advertising
Artist: **Milda Vizbar**
Art Director: Ned Harris/Milda Vizbar
Agency: Wallack & Harris, Inc.
Client: Tom Fields, Ltd.

368 Institutional
Artist: **Pete Turner**
Art Director: Pete Turner

369 Advertising
Artist: **Fred Marcellino**
Art Director: Andrew Kner
Client: The New York Times

370 Institutional
Artist: **Robert Byrd**
Art Director: Richard Mendelsohn
Client: American Artists

374 Television
Artist: **Ray Cruz**
Art Director: Dolores Gudzin
Client: NBC Television

373 Book
Artist: **Nicola Bayley**
Art Director: Lidia Ferrara
Title: The Tyger Voyage
Publisher: Alfred A. Knopf

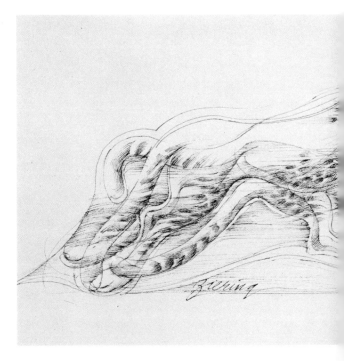

375 Editorial
Artist: **John Puchalski**
Art Director: John Puchalski

376 Book
Artist: **Nicholas Gaetano**
Art Director: Judith Loeser
Title: Celestial Omnibus
Publisher: Vintage Paperbacks

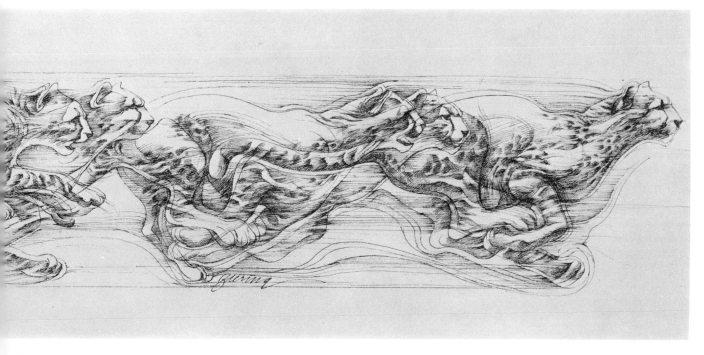

377 Advertising
Artist: **Bob Ziering**
Art Director: Howard Kates
Agency: N.W. Ayer ABH International
Client: T.V. Guide

378 Editorial
Artist: **James McMullan**
Art Director: Milton Glaser/Walter Bernard
Publication: New York Magazine

379 Editorial
Art: **Rick McCollum**
Art Director: John deCesare
Publication: Geigy Pharmaceuticals

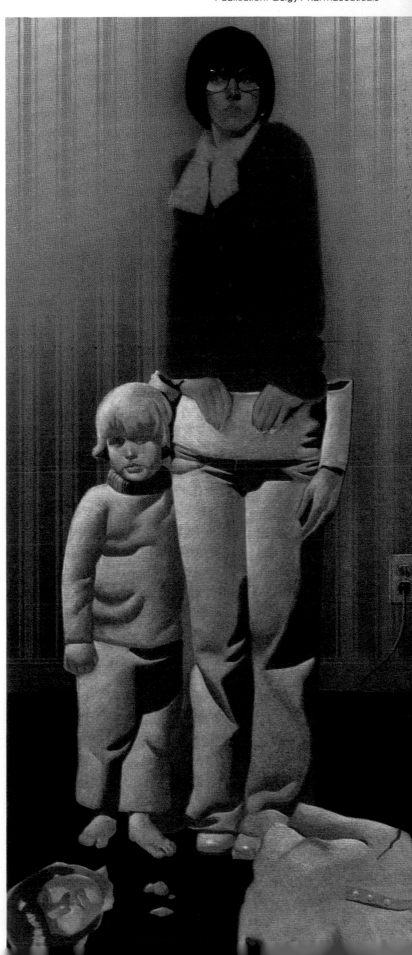

380 Book
Artist: **John Robinette**
Art Director: John Robinette

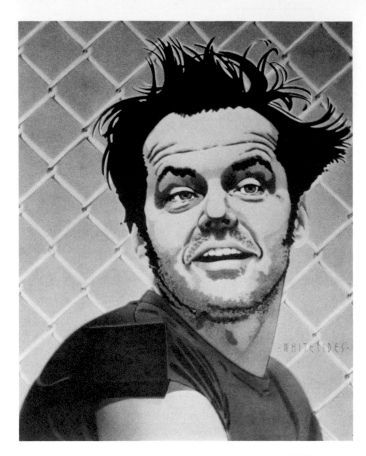

381 Editorial
Artist: **Kim Whitesides**
Art Director: Tony Lane
Publication: Rolling Stone

382 Institutional
Artist: **Bob Peak**
Art Director: Bob Peak
Client: Jack O'Grady Galleries, Inc.

383 Book
Artist: **Joanne Scribner**
Art Director: Paul Gamarello
Title: Elizabeth
Publisher: Random House

384 Book
Artist: **Barbara Weiss**
Art Director: Barbara Weiss

385 Institutional
Artist: **Jim Sharpe**
Art Director: Jim Sharpe

386 Book
Artist: **Daniel Maffia**
Art Director: Lidia Ferrara
Title: A New Life of Anton Chekhov
Publisher: Alfred A. Knopf

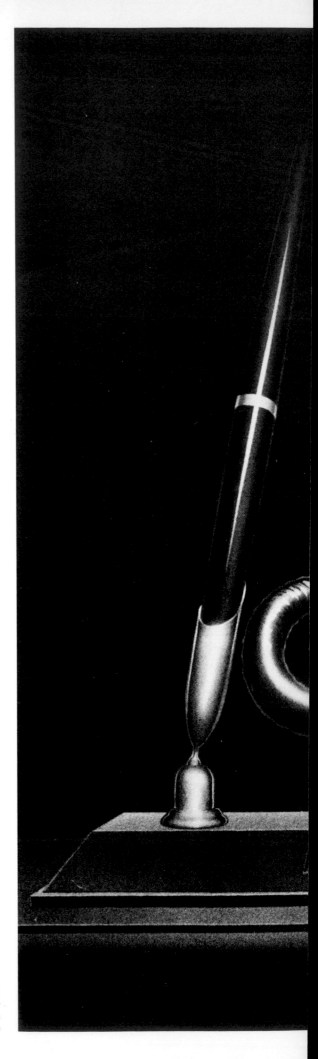

387 Editorial
Artist: **Vincent Topazio**
Art Director: Joe Brooks
Publication: Penthouse Magazine

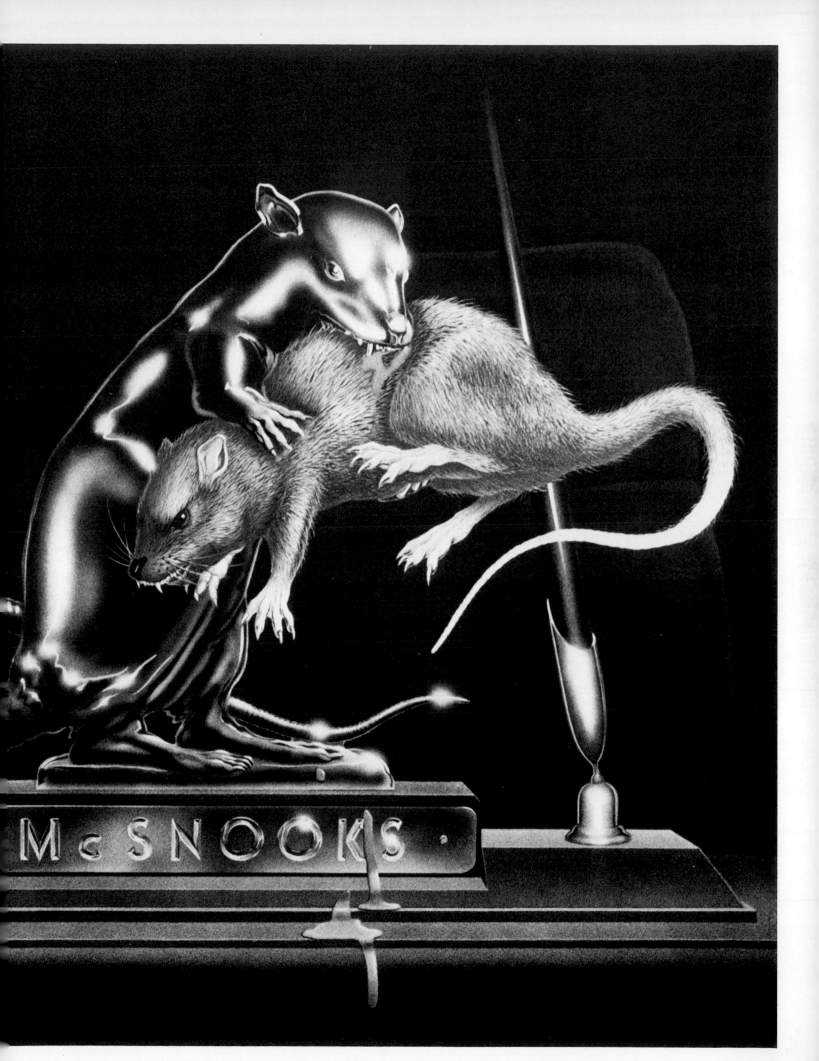

388 Television
Artist: **Annie Lunsford**
Art Director: Annie Lunsford
Agency: Churchmouse Graphics
Client: WRC-TV

389 Television
Artist: **Nicholas Gaetano**
Art Director: Sandy Carlson
Agency: Young & Rubicam
Client: Clairol

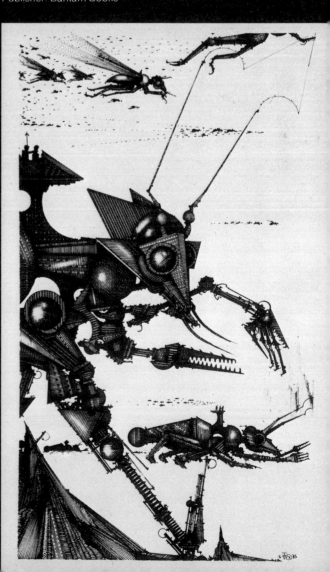

394 Editorial
Artist: **Daniel Schwartz**
Art Director: Lorraine M. Allen
Publication: Redbook Magazine

393 Editorial
Artist: **Bernard Fuchs**
Art Director: John Newcomb
Publication: Golf Digest

395 Institutional
Artist: **Stephen Durke**
Art Director: Stephen Durke/Larry McEntire
Client: Lonestar Studio

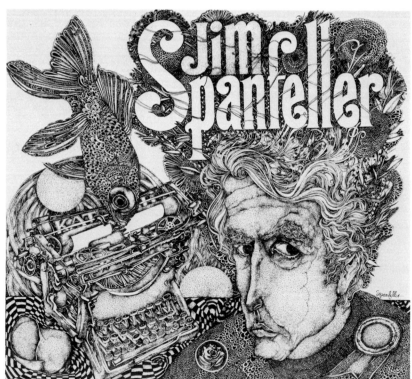

396 Institutional
Artist: **Jim Spanfeller**
Art Director: Tom Lennon
Client: Hydra

398 Advertising
Artist: **Jill Bossert**
Art Director: Jill Bossert

97 Book
tist: **Robert Grossman**
t Director: Ian Summers
le: No Left Turns
ublisher: Ballantine Books, Inc.

399 Advertising
Artist: **Robert T. Handville**
Art Director: Robert T. Handville
Client: Smithsonian Institution

400 Editorial
Artist: **Burt Silverman**
Art Director: Peter Christopher
Publication: MacLean's Magazine

403 Book
Artist: **Dennis Luzak**
Art Director: William Gregory
Title: The Tide Of Life
Publisher: Reader's Digest

404 Television
Artist: **Albino Hinojosa**
Art Director: Albino Hinojosa

405 Book
Artist: **Gil Cohen**
Art Director: Gil Cohen

406 Advertising
Artist: **Mark English**
Art Director: Jack O'Grady
Client: Jack O'Grady Galleries, Inc.

407 Institutional
Artist: **Ron Wolin**
Art Director: Ron Wolin/Keith Bright
Agency: Keith Bright & Associates
Client: Graphic Processing

408 Book
Artist: **Barbara Sandler**
Art Director: Atha Tehon
Title: Woman Chief
Publisher: The Dial Press

409 Advertising
Artist: **Rodica Prato**
Art Director: Bernard Vidal
Client: M.B.C. Advertising
Award For Excellence

410 Editorial
Artist: **Charles Santore**
Art Director: William Cadge
Publication: Redbook Magazine

411 Advertising
Artist: **Babette Marchand**
Art Director: Caroline Redden
Agency: Shaller Rubin Associates, Inc.
Client: Biagi, Division of Swank, Inc.

412 Book
Artist: **Ron Barrett**
Art Director: Riki Levinson
Title: Bible Stories You Can't Forget, No Matter
How Hard You Try
Publisher: E. P. Dutton & Co., Inc.

414 Editorial
Artist: **Siegbert Reinhard**
Art Director: Don Menell
Publication: Oui Magazine

413 Advertising
Artist: **Larry Weil**
Art Director: Larry Weil

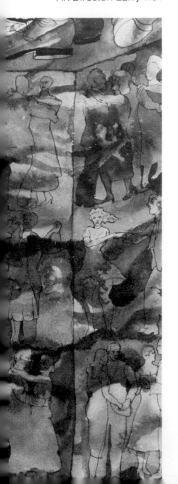

415 Advertising
Artist: **Vincent Petragnani**
Art Director: Dolores Gudzin
Client: NBC Television

417 Editorial
Artist: **Ned Seidler**
Art Director: Howard E. Paine
Publication: National Geographic Magazine

416 Editorial
Artist: **Bernard Fuchs**
Art Director: William Cadge
Publication: Redbook Magazine

418 Editorial
Artist: **Wilson McLean**
Art Director: David Merrill
Publication: Time Magazine

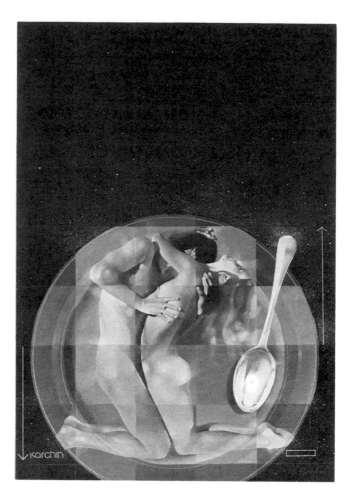

419 Book
Artist: **Steve Karchin**
Art Director: Ian Summers
Title: Money Is Love
Publisher: Ballantine Books, Inc.

422 Editorial
Artist: **George Sottung**
Art Director: George Sottung

421 Book
Artist: **Robert S. Brown**
Art Director: Robert S. Brown

420 Book
Artist: **Bernard Fuchs**
Art Director: Gordon Fisher
Title: The Scarlet Letter
Publisher: The Franklin Library

423 Editorial
Artist: **Ned Seidler**
Art Director: Howard E. Paine
Publication: National Geographic Magazine

424 Institutional
Artist: **Ray Wiley**
Art Director: Ray Wiley
Client: Mikulas Associates, Inc.

425 Editorial
Artist: **Bob Dacey**
Art Director: Sal Lazzorotti/Jessica Weber
Publication: Guideposts

426 Book
Artist: **Roland Descombes**
Art Director: Roland Descombes

427 Book
Artist: **Benjamin F. Stahl**
Art Director: Susan Meddaugh
Title: Freelon Starbird
Publisher; Houghton Mifflin Co.

428 Institutional
Artist: **Roy Andersen**
Art Director: Louann Ihde
Client: Louann Ihde

429 Editorial
Artist: **Bob Dacey**
Art Director: Herman Petras
Publication: Knave Magazine

431 Editorial
Artist: **Andris Leimanis**
Art Director: Hazel Lowe
Publication: Montreal Star

430 Advertising
Artist: **David Leffel**
Art Director: Richard Roth/Howard Smiley
Agency: Queens Graphics
Client: TK Records

432 Book
Artist: **Lew Friedland**
Art Director: Lew Friedland

433 Editorial
Artist: **James C. Christensen**
Art Director: James C. Christensen
Publication: New Era Magazine

434 Book
Artist: **Pam Ford**
Art Director: Pam Ford

435 Book
Artist: **Murray Tinkelman**
Art Director: Cathy Altholz/Bobye List
Title: Arctic
Publisher: Coward, McCann, Geohegan, Inc.

436 Institutional
Artist: **Nicholas Gaetano**
Art Director: Nicholas Gaetano
Client: Open Gallery Graphics

437 Book
Artist: **Jerry Pinkney**
Art Director: Jim Weren
Title: Anamsi and the Plantains
Publisher: Field Enterprises Educational Corp.

438 Editorial
Artist: **Craig Nelson**
Art Director: Art Aveilhe
Publication: Players Magazine

439 Institutional
Artist: **Stephen Tarantal**
Art Director: Bernie Karlin
Agency: AKM Associates, Inc.
Client: J. C. Penney Co., Inc.

440 Institutional
Artist: **Norman MacDonald**
Art Director: Andrew Kner
Client: Miranda & Kenneth Hine

441 Television
Artist: **Charles B. Slackman**
Art Director: Rod Capawana
Agency: Doremus & Co.
Client: Bank of New York

HANDKE
ERZÄHLT, WIE
DIE MOREAU
IHM ERZÄHLTE,
WIE...

443 Editorial
Artist: **John Collier**
Art Director: Modesto Torré
Publication: McCall's Magazine

444 Advertising
Artist: **Jacob Knight**
Art Director: Bob Heimall
Client: Arista Records

442 Editorial
Artist: **Jan Peter Tripp**
Art Director: Rainer Wörtmann
Publication: Playboy Germany

445 Book
Artist: **Wayne Anderson**
Art Director: Tom Maschler
Title: Ratsmagic
Publisher: Pantheon Books

446 Editorial
Artist: **Allan Mardon**
Art Director: Richard Gangel
Publication: Sports Illustrated

447 Editorial
Artist: **Stanley Meltzoff**
Art Director: Richard Gangel
Publication: Sports Illustrated

448 Editorial
Artist: **Roy LaGrone**
Art Director: Roy LaGrone
Client: Department of the Army/U.S. Center of
Military History

449 Editorial
Artist: **Stanley Metzoff**
Art Director: Richard Gangel
Publication: Sports Illustrated

450 Editorial
Artist: **Stan Hunter**
Art Director: Don Adamec
Publication: Ladies' Home Journal

451 Institutional
Artist: **Rainer Koenig**
Art Director: Rainer Koenig

452 Editorial
Artist: **Barron Storey**
Art Director: Lester Goodman
Publication: Rush Magazine

453 Editorial
Artist: **Burt Silverman**
Art Director: Neil Shakery
Publication: Psychology Today

454 Editorial
Artist: **Alan Magee**
Art Director: Joe Brooks
Publication: Penthouse Magazine

455 Book
Artist: **Jean-Leon Huens**
Art Director: Marion Davis
Title: Pride of the Peacock
Publisher: Reader's Digest

456 Institutional
Artist: **Mike Hodges**
Art Director: Mike Hodges

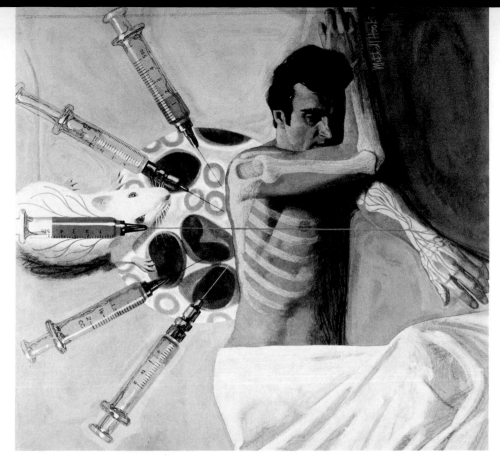

457 Editorial
Artist: **Mitchell Hooks**
Art Director: Howard Munce
Publication: Medical Times

458 Book
Artist: **Tom Hall**
Art Director: William Gregory
Title: The 10:30 From Marseille
Publisher: Reader's Digest

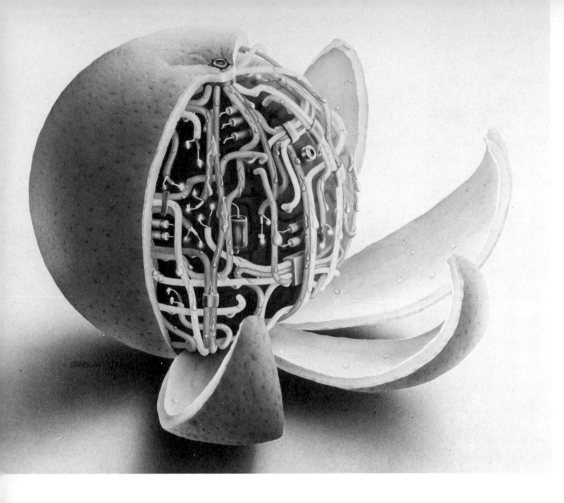

459 Advertising
Artist: **Stanislaw Fernandes**
Art Director: Ace Lehman
Client: RCA Records

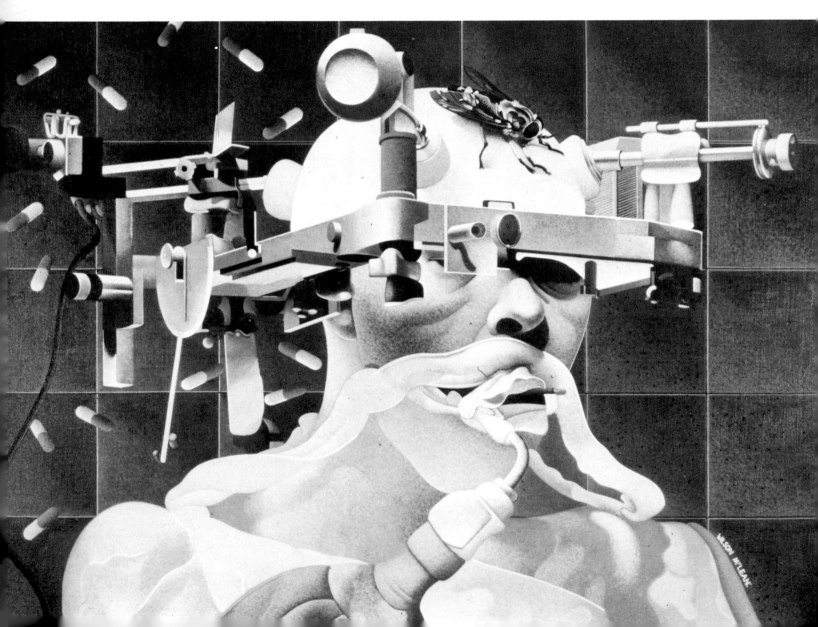

461 Institutional
Artist: **Etienne Delessert**
Art Director: Etienne Delessert
Client: Musée Des Arts Décoratifs

462 Advertising
Artist: **Etienne Delessert**
Art Director: Etienne Delessert
Client: Musée des Arts Décoratifs

460 Editorial
Artist: **Wilson McLean**
Art Director: Don Menell
Publication: Oui Magazine

463 Editorial
Artist: **C. Royd Crosthwaite**
Art Director: C. Royd Crosthwaite

464 Editorial
Artist: **John Berkey**
Art Director: John Berkey

465 Institutional
Artist: **John Berkey**
Art Director: Seth Huntington
Client: 3M Company

466 Editorial
Artist: **John Berkey**
Art Director: John Berkey

467 Editorial
Artist: **Louis S. Glanzman**
Art Director: Howard E. Paine
Publication: National Geographic Magazine

468 Institutional
Artist: **Dave Willardson/Joe Heiner/
Brian Zick**
Art Director: Pete Loehmeir/Kit Coorigan
Client: Leo Burnett Advertising Agency

469 Institutional
Artist: **Eugene Karlin**
Art Director: Ken Jordan
Client: Geigy Pharmaceuticals

470 Editorial
Artist: **Harvey Dinnerstein**
Art Director: Marjorie Glaubach
Publication: National Union of Hospital & Health
Care Employees

471 Book
Artist: **Harry J. Schaare**
Art Director: Harry J. Schaare

472 Institutional
Artist: **Eugene Karlin**
Art Director: Ken Jordan
Client: Geigy Pharmaceuticals

473 Advertising
Artist: **Robert Schulz**
Art Director: Fred Martin
Agency: Robert A. Becker, Inc.
Client: Roerig, Div. of Pfizer

nguorous shoreline, a
ow, on a July evening,
ntinued on page 118)

474 Editorial
Artist: **Walt Spitzmiller**
Art Director: Lorraine M. Allen
Publication: Redbook Magazine

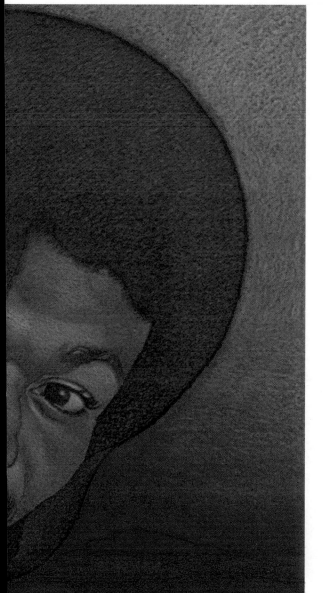

475 Advertising
Artist: **Charles Santore**
Art Director: Arnie Roberts
Client: WMOT Records

476 Editorial
Artist: **Robert Heindel**
Art Director: Richard Gangel
Publication: Sports Illustrated

477 Institutional
Artist: **Teresa Woodward**
Art Director: John G. Feldman
Agency: Brewer, Jones & Feldman, Inc.
Client: Beckett Paper Co.

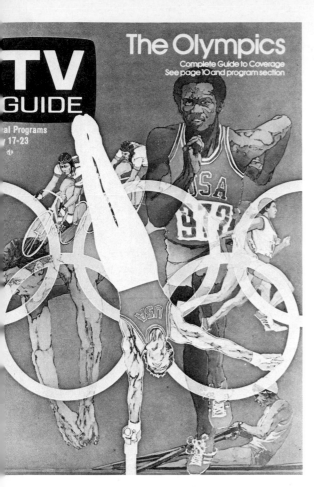

478 Editorial
Artist: **Jim Sharpe**
Art Director: Jerry Alten
Publication: T.V. Guide

479 Advertising
Artist: **Pat Nagel**
Art Director: Ernie Blitzer
Agency: Marsteller, Inc.
Client: Allied Chemical

480 Advertising
Artist: **Karen Laurence**
Art Director: Mike Withers
Client: Adtex, Inc.

481 Editorial
Artist: **Barron Storey**
Art Director: Leo McCarthy
Publication: Swank Magazine

481 Editorial
Artist: **Barron Storey**
Art Director: Leo McCarthy
Publication: Swank Magazine

Daydreaming—

482 Editorial
Artist: **Ellen Lyons**
Art Director: Dale Moyers
Publication: Science World

483 Advertising
Artist: **Babette Marchand**
Art Director: Caroline Redden
Agency: Shaller Rubin Associates, Inc.
Client: Biagi, Division of Swank, Inc.

484 Advertising
Artist: **Robert Heindel**
Art Director: Phillis Chillingworth
Client: Wamsutta

485 Advertising
Artist: **Karen Laurence**
Art Director: Mike Withers
Client: Adtex, Inc.

490 Advertising
Artist: **Stanislaw Fernandes**
Art Director: Dick Smith
Client: RCA Records

489 Editorial
Artist: **Richard Harvey**
Art Director: Linda Cox
Publication: Cosmopolitan

491 Book
Artist: **San Julian**
Art Director: John Van Zwienen
Title: Traitor's Son
Publisher: Dell Publishing Co.

492 Book
Artist: **Charles Lilly**
Art Director: Jean Krulis
Title: The Peppermint Pig
Publisher: J. B. Lippincott Co.

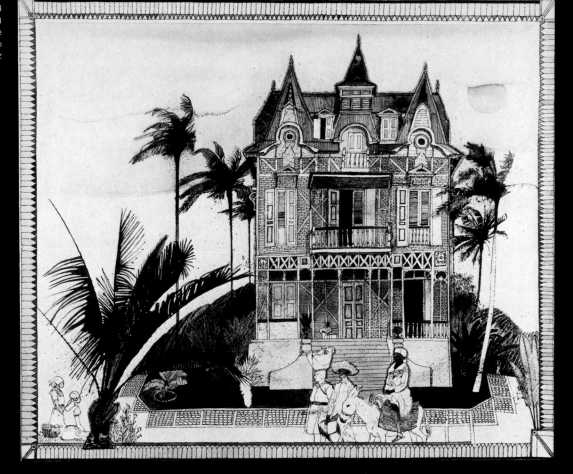

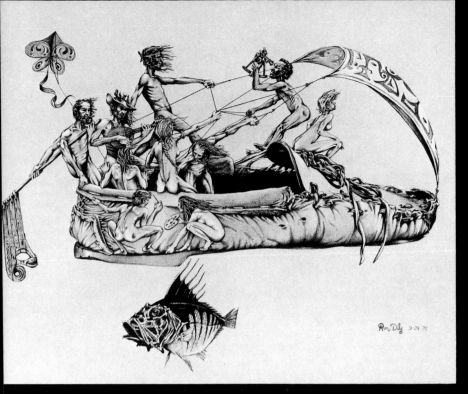

499 Book
Artist: **Tom Upshur**
Art Director: James Plumeri
Title: Elton John
Publisher: New American Library

498 Advertising
Artist: **Barron Storey**
Art Director: Alan Davis
Client: London Records

500 Book
Artist: **Simms Taback**
Art Director: Mildred Kantrowitz
Title: Euphonia and the Flood
Publisher: Parents Magazine Press

501 Book
Artist: **Tony Chen**
Art Director: Joseph Taney
Title: A Day in the Woods
Publisher: National Geographic Society

502 Book
Artist: **Tony Chen**
Art Director: Joseph Taney
Title: A Day in the Woods
Publisher: National Geographic Society

503 Television
Artist: **Jon C. McIntosh**
Art Director: Mac Acosta
Client: Media Systems Corp.

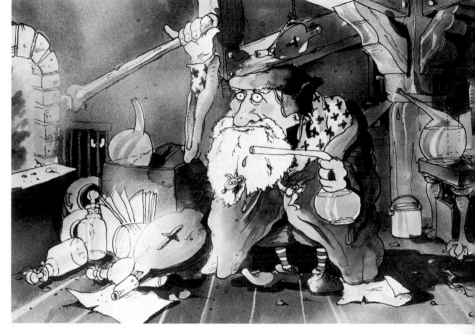

504 Institutional
Artist: **Carol Wald**
Art Director: Carol Wald

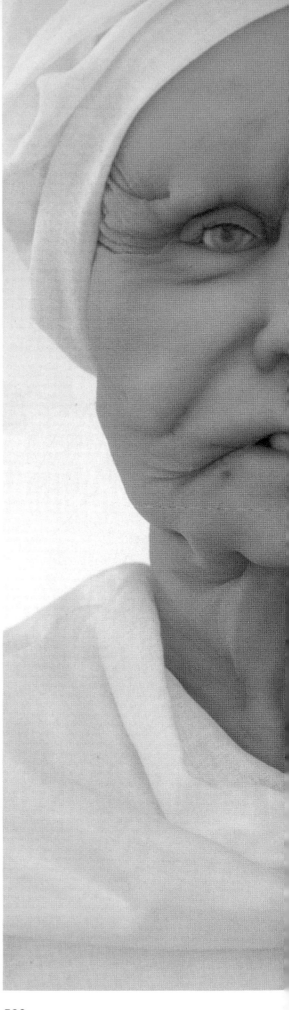

505 Editorial
Artist: **Wilson McLean**
Art Director: Joe Brooks
Publication: Penthouse Magazine

506 Editorial
Artist: **Judith Jampel**
Art Director: Rowan Johnson
Publication: Viva Magazine

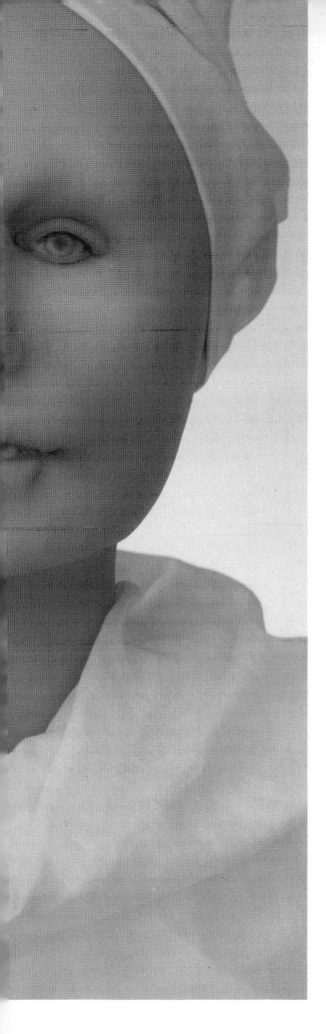

507 Advertising
Artist: **David Jarvis**
Art Director: Peter Whorf
Client: ABC Dunhill Records

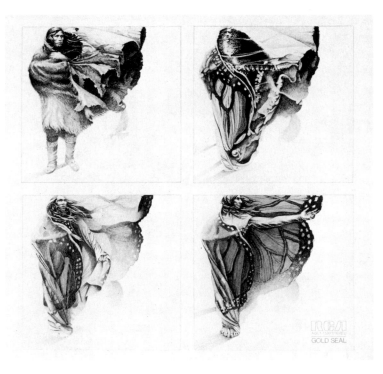

512 Editorial
Artist: **Eraldo Carugati**
Art Director: Arthur Paul
Publication: Playboy

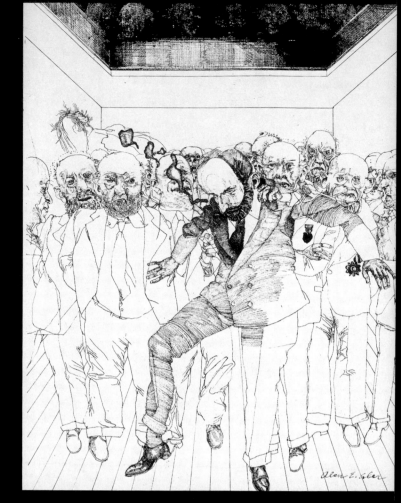

513 Advertising
Artist: **Robert Weaver**
Art Director: Alan J. Klawans
Client: Smith, Kline & French Laboratories

514 Book
Artist: **Donna Diamond**
Art Director: Jane Zalben
Title: The Boy Who Sang The Birds
Publisher: Charles Scribner's Sons

515 Book
Artist: **Alan E. Cober**
Art Director: David Glixsen
Title: The Trial
Publisher: Limited Editions Book Club

516 Book
Artist: **Alan E. Cober**
Art Director: David Glixsen
Title: The Trial
Publisher: Limited Editions Book Club

517 Book
Artist: **Paul Giovanopoulos**
Art Director: Alan Benjamin
Title: Learning to Say Good-By
Publisher: Macmillan Publishing Co., Inc.

518 Institutional
Artist: **Paul Giovanopoulos**
Art Director: Paul Giovanopoulos

519 Book
Artist: **David Grove**
Art Director: Leonard Leone.
Title: Captain Blood
Publisher: Bantam Books

520 Institutional
Artist: **Murray Tinkelman**
Art Director: Murray Tinkelman
Client: Warlock Press

521 Editorial
Artist: **Larry A. Gerber**
Art Director: Seymour Gerber
Agency: G/D Advertising, Inc.
Client: Braniff International

522 Institutional
Artist: **Jane Sterrett**
Art Director: Jane Sterrett

523 Advertising
Artist: **Robert Giusti**
Art Director: Bob Defrin/Abie Sussman
Client: Atlantic Records

Illustrators

INDEX

19

ILLUSTRATORS

Acuña, Ed, 180
462 Riverside Avenue
Westport, CT

Almquist, Don, 390
166 Grovers Avenue
Bridgeport, CT

Ameijide, Raymond, 316
251 East 51 Street
New York City

Andersen, Roy, 171, 248, 249,
   265, 428
2 Apricot Lane
Ridgefield, CT

Anderson, Wayne, 328, 347, 445
c/o Jonathan Cape Ltd.
30 Bedford Square
London WC1, England

Anthony, Carol, 315, 343
123 Byram Shore Road
Greenwich, CT

Bandoian, Catherine, 312
4461 West 4 Street, #205
Los Angeles, CA

Bang, Molly Garrett, 336
Box 299 Water Street
Woodshole, MA

Barrett, Ron, 412, 497
344 West 72 Street
New York City

Bascove, Barbara, 72, 110
1 University Place
New York City

Bass, Marilyn, 245
R.D. 3, Gipsy Trail Road
Carmel, NY

Bayley, Nicola, 373
16 Chalcot Gardens
England's Lane
London NW3, England

Becker, Ron, 6
265 East 78 Street
New York City

Bennett, Elizabeth, 268, 269
36 East 23 Street
New York City

Berkey, John, 351, 464, 465, 466
c/o Frank & Jeff Lavaty
45 East 51 Street
New York City

Billout, Guy, 85, 333
222 West 15 Street
New York City

Blake, Quentin, 494
c/o Ted Riley
252 East 49 Street
New York City

Bonner, Lee, 277
2613 Maryland Avenue
Baltimore, MD

Bordelon, Melinda, 118
138 Mountain Road
Cornwall, NY

Bossert, Jill, 226, 398
154 East 64 Street
New York City

Brofsky, Miriam, 292
186 Riverside Drive
New York City

Brown, Robert S., 421
221 Erlanger Boulevard
North Babylon, NY

Butte, Annie, 327, 330
P.O. Box 180
Jacksonville, OR

Byrd, Robert, 15, 370
409 Warwick Road
Haddonfield, NJ

Campbell, Jim, 18, 319
485 North Main Street
Westport, CT

Carugati, Eraldo, 329, 334, 512
1567 Ridge
Evanston, IL

Cason, Merrill, 1
341 East 87 Street
New York City

Chen, Tony, 501, 502
53-31 96 Street
Corona, NY

Chorao, Kay, 159
290 Riverside Drive
New York City

Christensen, Dave, 243
328 West 19 Street
New York City

Christensen, James C., 210, 433
490 N 800 East
American Fork, UT

Chung, Hau-Chee, 124
19 South Evergreen
Memphis, TN

Chwast, Seymour, 91
Pushpin Studio
207 East 32 Street
New York City

Cober, Alan E., 32, 50, 222, 364,
   515, 516
Croton Dam Road
Ossining, NY

CoConis, Ted, 4, 51, 59, 196, 214
145 East 69 Street
New York City

Cohen, Gil, 405
350 East Willow Grove
Philadelphia, PA

Collier, John, 22, 296, 443
North Quaker Hill Road
Pauling, NY

Colonna, Bernard P., 241
1230 Bloomfield Street
Hoboken, NJ

Condak, Cliff, 262, 509
Moffett Road
Cold Spring, NY

Cooper, Heather, 77, 221, 259
96 Bloor Street
Toronto, Ontario, Canada

Corson, Richard, 125
536 Johnston Drive
Watchung, NJ

Cosgrove, Jerry L., 363
206 East 38 Street
New York City

Craft, Kinuko Y., 153
2007 North Cleveland
Chicago, IL

Crosthwaite, C. Royd, 463
c/o Frank & Jeff Lavaty
45 East 51 Street
New York City

Cruz, Ray, 374
c/o V. Morgan
194 Third Avenue
New York City

Cunningham, Robert M., 365
177 Waverly Place
New York City

Dacey, Bob, 240, 246, 247,
   425, 429
P.O. Box 137
Redding, CT

David, Cyril, 27, 127
135 Hog Creek Road
East Hampton, NY

Davis, Paul, 152
Rector Street
Sag Harbor, NY

Delessert, Etienne, 39, 76, 176,
   339, 461, 462
c/o Newbourne
135 East 54 Street
New York City

Descombes, Roland, 426
c/o Frank & Jeff Lavaty
45 East 51 Street
New York City

Diamond, Donna, 514
312 West 88 Street
New York City

Dilg, Ron, 495
509 West 54 Street
New York City

Dillon, Diane, 300
221 Kane Street
Brooklyn, NY

Dillon, Leo, 300
221 Kane Street
Brooklyn, NY

Dinnerstein, Harvey, 28, 121, 470
933 President Street
Brooklyn, NY

Downey, William, 69
21 Vista Place
Red Bank, NJ

Durbin, Mike, 348
4034 Woodcraft
Houston, TX

Sundgaard, Erik, 155
821 Cornwall Avenue
Cheshire, CT

Szafran, Gene, 326
RD #3, Old Redding Road
West Redding, CT

Taback, Simms, 500
38 East 21 Street
New York City

Tarantal, Stephen, 439
7007 North 12 Street
Philadelphia, PA

Tauss, Herb, 197
South Mountain Pass
Garrison, NY

Thompson, John, 23, 116, 237
171 Duane Street
New York City

Tinkelman, Murray, 193, 284,
303, 435, 520
75 Lakeview Avenue West
Peekskill, NY

Topazio, Vincent, 387
16 North Astor Street
Irvington, NY

Toulmin-Rothe, Ann, 140
c/o Publishers Graphics
611 Riverside Avenue
Westport, CT

Tripp, Jan Peter, 442
Reinsburg Strasse 53
8982 Tiefenbach, Germany

Turner, Pete, 368
938 Pamlico Drive
Cary, NC

Unruh, Jack, 123, 493, 496
333 7616 LBJ
Dallas, TX

Upshur, Tom, 499
20 Perarsal Place
Roslyn Heights, NY

Viskupic, Gary, 287
7 Westfield Drive
Center Port, NY

Vizbar, Milda, 367
529 East 84 Street
New York City

Wald, Carol, 504
182 Grand Street
New York City

Waldrep, Richard, 107
c/o Whistling Dixie
200 East 58 Street
New York City

Walker, Norm, 294
282 Newtown Avenue
Norwalk, CT

Wallner, John C., 366
19 Seneca Road
Ossining, NY

Walters, Candace, 3
c/o Carol Bancroft
185 Good Hill Road
Weston, CT

Warhol, Andy, 16
c/o Fred Hughes
Andy Warhol Enterprises
860 Broadway
New York City

Warren, Dave, 13
2186 Victory Parkway
Cincinnati, OH

Weaver, Norman, 309
c/o Artists Partners
14-18 Ham Yard
London, England

Weaver, Robert, 508, 513
42 East 12 Street
New York City

Weill, Larry, 413
421 East 81 Street
New York City

Weiss, Barbara, 384
23856 Norcrest
Southfield, MI

White, Jim, 304
230 East Ohio
Chicago, IL

Whitesides, Kim, 381
1 West 85 Street
New York City

Wilcox, David, 45, 185
c/o Rabin & Newborn
135 East 54 Street
New York City

Wiley, Ray, 424
3408 Morier Street
Jacksonville, FL

Willardson, David, 92, 468
Star Studios
2224 Ponet Drive
Los Angeles, CA

Williams, Ronald, 41
5217 Raphael Street
Los Angeles, CA

Wohlberg, Ben, 104
43 Great Jones Street
New York City

Wolfe, Bruce, 231,239
206 El Cerrito Avenue
Piedmont, CA

Wolin, Ron, 407
3977 Oeste Avenue
Studio City, CA

Woodward, Teresa, 477
544 Paseo Miramar
Pacific Palisades, CA

Zick Brian, 468
Star Studios
2224 Ponet Drive
Los Angeles, CA

Ziering, Bob, 26, 126, 189, 377
151 West 74 Street
New York City

ART DIRECTORS

Acosta, Mal, 503
Adamec, Don, 129, 320, 450
Adell, Judith, 26
Allen, Lorraine M., 394, 474
Almquist, Don, 390
Alten, Jerry, 7, 317, 478
Altholz, Cathy, 193, 435
Alvis, Horalto, 164
Anderson, Betty, 252
Apilado, Tony, 12
Atkinson, Jack, 228
Aveilhe, Art, 263, 438

Baker, Dick, 90
Bandoian, Catherine, 312
Barry, Jim, 10
Bartels, David, 158, 239
Bass, Marilyn, 245
Benjamin, Alan, 336, 517
Benoit, Dennis, 496
Berg, John, 161, 173, 251, 508
Berkey, John, 351, 464, 466
Bernard, Walter, 28, 121, 378
Bertoli, Barbara, 98, 162, 203, 213
230
Black, Roger, 29
Blitzer, Ernie, 479
Bloedow, William L., 319
Blum, Chris, 231
Bond, Bill, 123
Bossert, Jill, 226, 398
Bradley, Nancy, 266
Bran, Stuart, 118
Bright, Keith, 138, 407
Brooks, Joe, 111, 115, 185, 216,
227, 267, 345, 387, 454, 505
Brown, Richard D., 168
Brown, Robert S., 421
Burns, Robert, 259
Butte, Bruce, 327, 330

Cadge, William, 204, 206, 410, 416
Campbell, Ronald, 225
Capawana, Rod, 283, 441
Carlson, Sandy, 389
Carson, Carol, 209
Caserta, Joe, 277
Catalano, Al, 234
Chaikin, Miriam, 359
Chapman, Barbara, 136
Charles, Milton, 86, 310
Chillingworth, Phillis, 484
Christensen, James C., 210, 433
Christopher, Peter, 400
Clarke, Grace, 260
Closi, Victor J., 255
Cohen, Gil, 405
Condak, Cliff, 262
Condak, Henrietta, 46, 47, 173,
262, 509
Connolly, Joe, 100, 240
Connolly, Joseph, 256
Cooper, Heather, 77, 221
Coorigan, Kit, 468
Coro, Ron, 195
Costello, Bo, 32
Cox, Linda, 4, 489
Crosthwaite, C. Royd, 463
Csatari, Joe, 346

Dacey, Bob, 247
Danbrot, Bruce, 320
Daniels, Frank, 402
David, Cyril, 27, 127

Davis, Alan, 128, 215, 498
Davis, Marion, 455
deCesare, John, 379
Defrin, Bob, 45, 91, 518
Delessert, Etienne, 39, 76, 176,
339, 461, 462
Demoney, Jerry, 116
Descombes, Roland, 426
DeVito, Frank, 126
Diamond, Harry O., 207, 494
Dilg, Ron, 495
Draper, Edythe, 233
Durbin, Mike, 348
Durke, Stephen, 395
Dykstra, Phillip, 319

Edwards, Roxanne, 51
Eubanks, Tony, 141, 182

Farrell, Richard, 201
Faure, Renee, 109
Feldgus, Bob, 63, 261
Feldman, John G., 477
Ferrara, Lidia, 69, 306, 373, 386
Fisher, Gordon, 420
Foley, Jack, 360
Foley, Mike, 148
Ford, Pam, 434
Foti, Albert M., 30
Frank, David, 52
Friedland, Lew, 432
Friedman, Stan, 163, 178, 179
Fury, Len, 49, 144

Gaetano, Nicholas, 436
Gallardo, Gervasio, 325
Gamarello, Paul, 175, 383
Gangel, Richard, 8, 43, 50, 99,
134, 142, 165, 364, 446, 447,
449, 476
Gardiner, Cliff, 287
Geissmann, Robert, 318
Geller, Martin, 120
Gerber, Seymour, 280, 521
Gilbert, Barbara, 11
Giovanopoulos, Paul, 270, 518
Gist, Linda E., 157
Glaser, Milton, 121, 378
Glaubach, Marjorie, 470
Glixsen, David, 515, 516
Gold, Bill, 249
Goldman, Marvin, 245
Goodman, Lester, 322, 452
Gotfryd, Alex, 243
Graham, Mariah, 391
Green, Bert, 64
Gregory, William, 74, 102, 103,
119, 199, 295,321 403, 458
Grossman, Alvin, 62, 117, 149
Grote, Rich, 66
Gudzin, Dolores, 17, 18, 374, 415

Hall, Bruce W., 55, 335
Hancock, Wade, 67
Handville, Robert T., 339
Harris, Ned, 367
Hartzell, Dave, 95
Hau-Chee Chung, 124
Heck, John, 58
Hedden, Jim, 171
Heimall, Bob, 81, 289, 333, 444
Heller, Steve, 73, 258
Hennessy, Barbara, 366
Hinojosa, Albino, 404
Hodges, Mike, 456
Hoffner, Marilyn, 19
Holiday, Linda, 101

CLIENTS

TITLES

Illustrators

PRODUCTION CREDITS

The type in this book is
Helvetica medium and light
Composition by
M. J. Baumwell, Typography
Offset plates and printing by
Connecticut Printers, Inc.
The paper is
Mead's Black and White Offset Enamel Dull
Paper supplier
Andrews/Nelson/Whitehead Publishing Papers
Binding by
A. Horowitz and Son
Jacket printed by
Princeton Polychrome Press
Production Supervision
Lee Tobin, Hastings House
Assistant to the publisher
James Moore, Hastings House

Realistic art and art styles Imitated by
artist: Raymond Kursár

One Lincoln Plaza-New York, N.Y. 10023
To view Portfolio call (212) 873-5605

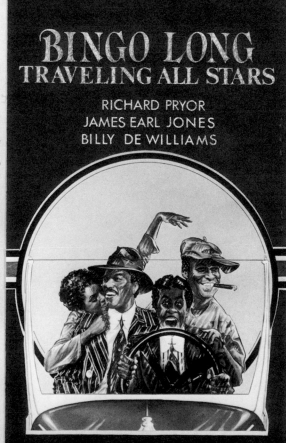

We hope you'll drop in on us whenever you're in the Washington
area. We like visitors, and we'd enjoy showing you our new home.

Time-Life Books Inc.
777 Duke Street
Alexandria, Va. 22314
Tel: (703) 960-5200

Behind the truly outstanding art you'l

nd Frank and Jeff Lavaty.

You'll find contemporary and nostalgic styles treating all subjects. Individual portfolios are available from the following artists represented exclusively by Frank and Jeff Lavaty.

John Berkey, Don Daily, Bernard D'Andrea, Roland Descombes, Chris Duke, Gervasio Gallardo, Martin Hoffman, Stan Hunter, Chet Jezierski, David McCall Johnston, Mort Kunstler, Lemuel Line, Robert Logrippo, Charles Moll, Carlos Ochagavia, Robert Schulz. Representative booklet of 100 color examples available for your file. Phone (212) 355-0910. Or write Frank and Jeff Lavaty, 45 East 51st St., N.Y., N.Y. 10022.

ART & ILLUSTRATION

ART

FRANK & JEFF LAVATY—ARTIST REPRESENTATIVES
45 EAST 51st STREET, N.Y., N.Y. 22. PHONE 212-355-0910

Pitt
Studios
is
open
minded

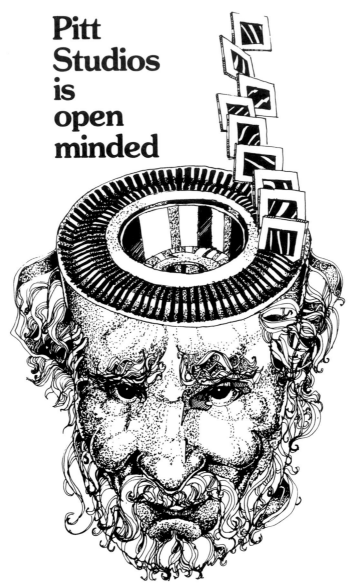

We'd like to see what you've
done and try to guess what
you're going to do.

Pitt Studios — biggest in
Cleveland, biggest in Pittsburgh
— would like to screen your
samples. Maybe you're the
designer or illustrator
we're looking for.

Pitt Studios
Art/Design/Communication
Cleveland: 216-241-6720
1370 Ontario Street 44113
Pittsburgh: 412/261-0460
Four Gateway Center 15222

Phone us collect if you've
got good news for us.

Are you this happy when you finish an art job?

Some artists are!

They're dancing for dough—by asking realistic prices for their creative work. The serious artist must keep abreast of the changing times and the prices one can demand today. One of the best ways to do this is to have a copy of the only artwork price guide on the market.

We take our business seriously!

The revised and enlarged 1978 edition of the Graphic Artists Guild PRICING AND ETHICAL GUIDELINES is a comprehensive guide to fair prices and business practices in every area of the graphic arts. It was compiled by practicing artists who are authorities in their special areas. It is the set of standards and the Code of Ethics officially accepted and adhered to by the Graphic Artists Guild—standards which the Guild feels should guide practices throughout the graphic arts industry.

PRICING AND ETHICAL GUIDE-LINES also covers such subjects as:
- How to deal with inflation
- Re-use and extended use of artwork
- Formulas for pricing through consideration of print orders
- Outright purchase vs reproduction rights
- How to deal with inordinate expenses and unusual time demands
- Analysis of the new copyright law: how it affects artists' ownership rights and client relationships

Price: $8.00 per copy, or $5.50 per copy for orders of 10 or more (postage and sales tax are included). Send check or money order to GRAPHIC ARTISTS GUILD, 30 E. 20th St., Rm. 405, New York, New York 10003. (Invoice orders accepted only for 10 or more copies.) Free to members of the Graphic Artists Guild—membership information sent upon request.

Also available from the Guild:
The second annual Graphic Artists Guild TALENT DIRECTORY. This catalog contains samples of artwork and biographies of several hundred Guild member artists. The disciplines include Graphic Designers, Illustrators, Textile Designers, Book and Book Jacket Designers, Medical Illustrators, Technical Designers and Illustrators, Fashion Designers and Illustrators—and a large variety of other disciplines. It is a valuable reference source for art directors and artwork buyers.

The Guild Directory is distributed free of charge to over 5,000 major art buyers throughout the United States. If you wish to receive a free copy please write on your company letterhead to the GRAPHIC ARTISTS GUILD, 30 E. 20th St., Rm. 405, New York, New York 10003.

artists

Norman Adams, Robert Heindel,
Gillian Hills, Dick Krepel,
Norman LaLiberte, Dennis Luzak,
John Martin, Rick McCollum,
Richard Newton, Fred Otnes,
Gene Szafran.

Represented by:
Bill Erlacher, Artists Associates
211 East 51 Street, New York, N.Y. 10022
Telephone: (212) 755-1365/6
Associates: Arlene Reiss,
Madeline Renard

JESSIE NEELEY

JESSIE NEELEY ARTIST REPRESENTATIVE 575-1234

art staff inc.

Advertising Art

369 Lexington Avenue
New York, N.Y. 10017
Tel. (212) 867-2660

OUR TEN COMMANDMENTS of ARTIST REPRESENTATION

1. We represent only artists we believe in and are totally committed to them.

2. We believe in being more than agents and become involved in the *total career* of the artists we represent.

3. We appreciate the problems of the artist and try, whenever possible, to alleviate these problems.

4. We also appreciate the problems of the art director: his client-agency relationship, tight deadlines and budget limitations and try to help him solve these problems whenever we can.

5. We believe in *full representation*. That means taking on only that number of artists that we can fully represent as well as insuring that each artist is non-competitive in style with other artists we represent.

6. We believe in giving *full service* to our artists and to the art director, promptly and professionally. Every client, no matter what the job price, deserves the very best we can offer.

7. We believe in being *flexible*. Business conditions change. The economy rises and falls. Accounts switch. We and our artists must adjust to all changes in order to successfully survive.

8. We believe in always meeting deadlines and always keeping a bargain. We and our artists are only as good as our word and our last job.

9. We believe in *BEING HONEST* at all times. With our artists. With the art director. With ourselves.

10. And finally, we believe in our *profession* ... the profession of representing artists. We firmly believe that it is the most exciting and challenging profession anywhere and we are proud to be a part of it.

Barbara & Elliott Gordon

Barbara Gordon
Associates Ltd.
165 East 32 Street
New York, N.Y. 10016
212-686-3514

ROY MILLER, JR.
ILLUSTRATOR

5378 HAZELHURST STREET • PHILADELPHIA, PENNSYLVANIA 19131

Representing
Over 30 Illustrators
Specializing In
Children's Materials

Contact
Carol Bancroft
185 Goodhill Road
Weston Connecticut 06883
203·226·7674

If you want to work side by side with greatest illustrators, read this:

by Nick Meglin

In the summer of 1976 American Artist Magazine asked me to write an article about a new enterprise, The Illustrators Workshop, a concentrated one month illustration program put together by 7 well-known leaders in the field. I attended the workshop in order to witness the program. I visited The Workshop again in the summer of 1977 as a guest speaker. This second visit enabled me to have "one-to-one" exchanges with the students. I learned that several major companies such as Hallmark Cards and Maritz Motivation Corporation were so pleased with what the workshop had done for several of their employees that first summer that they sponsored more of their people in this second year.

I was impressed by the response of the new group as I had been a year earlier with the charter members. Also impressive was the attitude of Michael Smollin, Managing Director, and the 6 illustrators whose names and reputations were obviously the prime attraction for most enrolees. Rather than simply repeat a course of study that had proven successful the year before, the faculty used what they had learned to strengthen, enrich and broaden the scope of The Workshop. Other than that, I found little to add to the original article, the essence of which follows:

What has been missing from the field of illustration for too long a time is the opportunity for an apprenticeship stage, that period of time in a career which has served an important role in the development of many exceptional illustrators in the past. Howard Pyle's famed "Brandywine School" provided that opportunity for the likes of N. C. Wyeth, Harvey Dunn and Maxfield Parrish. The apprenticeship idea continued through to the 50s when the big studios offered many fledgling illustrators the chance to develop under the watchful eyes of that decade's stars. Since then the steady demise of the studio system has forced the novice to learn and develop alone in his studio, being limited by his singular experience.

Aware of this unfortunate situation, six of

America's greatest illustrators conceived The Illustrators Workshop in 1976. The names of these six illustrators are a *Who's Who* of contemporary American illustration. They are Alan E. Cober, Mark English, Bernie Fuchs, Bob Heindel, Fred Otnes and Robert Peak. In turn, they persuaded Michael J. Smollin, a fellow illustrator who also had distinguished experience in advertising and management, to become Managing Director. Together these seven men put together a program that was simple and straightforward. The immediate success of their program indicates the need for advanced illustration students to work alongside already established and enterprising illustrators.

The Illustrators Workshop finally evolved into a one-month-per-year intensive training course. Can any institution exist on such a short-term basis? "It has to and does," offers Director Smollin. "If you're going to use top artists, you can't involve them for greater lengths of time because they have their own careers to think about. It's rare when you can get the *doers* to do the teaching. It's even rarer to find such great talent who can also teach so well! This opportunity is obviously filling a need for young illustrators. But some applicants admit that they are, in fact, intimidated by the instructors' reputations and by the high caliber of accepted students. We earnestly try to make them realize the importance of self-assurance. We all devote a great deal of attention throughout each program to building the students' confidence. After all, they are

six of America's

anning to compete in a very tough marketplace."

Have the students actually gained by the experience of working with the Illustrators? Private interviews, with randomly chosen students, confirmed that the Workshop's concept is valid. These students soon learned that Fuchs was Fuchs, English was English, ober was Cober, and that their best chance for succeeding in the field was in being themselves, not a facsimile of someone else. They were gratified that they had been discouraged from imitation, a difficult challenge for those who had chosen to study with an illustrator whose work they had so admired. The students were forced to take chances and get outside of themselves; that certainly left its mark as evidenced in so many comments.

"The way all of the instructors had of being so honest and open really knocked me out. They gave so much of themselves and yet they were always sensitive my needs and problems."

"The Workshop was one of the highlights of my life because everyone dealt with me with such gut-vel honesty. The piece I did for the *Playboy* assignment was my finest piece of art. I don't know that I ould have achieved it without The Workshop help d experience."

"I feel my art was genuinely appreciated and I restored and inspired because of this."

The Illustrators Workshop program is comprised of two important segments: The Seminar, a one week series of lectures by the instructors, leading magazine art directors, and corporate graphic designers, open to all buyers, sellers and doers of illustration; The Workshop, devoted to working on the assignments, the culmination of all the discussions, photo sessions, planning stages and research.

Since assignments are, obviously, what the world of illustration is all about, The Illustrators Workshop relies on real assignments for the proper learning experience. It enables the student to react under professional conditions and exposes him to a large variety of approaches in solving the same problem. This experience helps the student build his individuality and greater creativity. Each student receives daily individual attention from the members of the faculty. These vital one-to-one "crits" are given in the classrooms, the lecture halls and even the students dorm rooms. The finished work has impressed the guest art directors. In the past two years, they have come to The Workshop to give their assignments and have returned to review each piece that was done. Some of these outstanding guests were Art Paul, Art Director of Playboy magazine, Neil Shakery, former Art Director of Psychology Today magazine and Eugene Light, Art Director of Warner Books. The original concept of this program—the instructor and student work side-by-side, just as they might have in earlier times—is as valid today as it was years ago.

Alan E. Cober, President of The Illustrators Workshop, points out that people who apply for the annual Workshop programs thereby show signs of the dedication and determination necessary to succeed in this field. As he says, "Taking a chance is important. It's the first step toward reaching one's goal."

If *you* want to work side by side with six of America's greatest illustrators in 1978, write to:
Michael J. Smollin, Managing Director
The Illustrator's Workshop / The Seminar
Box 280, Easton, Conn. 06425

"Six Famous Americans" by Six Famous Illustrators

The Committee for The Picture Collection of the New York Public Library presents a portfolio of prints by The Illustrators Workshop, Inc.: Alan E. Cober, Mark English, Bernie Fuchs, Bob Heindel, Fred Otnes, Robert Peak

"Custer" by Robert Peak

"Louis Armstrong" by Bernie Fuchs

"Mathew Brady" by Mark English

"Aaron Copland" by Alan E. Cober

"Martha Graham" by Bob Heindel

"P.T. Barnum" by Fred Otnes

The Picture Collection of the New York Public Library has been the mainstay of picture researchers, artists, designers and countless others in the visual fields for so many years that it has come to be taken for granted. It is the largest, free, circulating picture library in the country—over two million images ranging in categories from Aardvark (Animals) to Zenobia (Personalities.) But like all other aspects of New York City services it has fallen upon evil financial days.

In a typical New York fashion, a band of public-spirited citizens who used the Collection came together last year to do what they could to put it back on its feet. The Committee For The Picture Collection, Inc. is composed of persons professionally involved in the arts, publishing, stagecraft, textile design and television. We have been functioning since 1976 as an independent fund-raising operation for this very important Collection. This year we would like to express our appreciation to The Illustrators Workshop, Inc. for their initiation of this project. Our special thanks to Alan E. Cober, President; Mark English; Bernard Fuchs; Bob Heindel; Fred Otnes; Robert Peak and Michael J. Smollin, Managing Director. Their generosity and support will help the Collection continue its operation.

Any contribution you can make either as a professional in any of the visual fields, or as an interested citizen, will go ultimately toward helping produce more works of a similar outstanding quality.

We are pleased to be able to offer this set of six 12″ x 12″ prints. These portraits are admirably suited for framing and are presented in an elegant portfolio.

Make checks payable to:

Committe for the Picture Collection, Inc.
N.Y. Public Library, Room 73
Fifth Avenue and 42nd Street
New York, N.Y. 10018

Please send me the portfolio edition(s) indicated below.

For Members	For Non-members
Unsigned edition ....$10.	Unsigned edition............$15.
Signed edition.................$25.	Signed edition.................$30.

The signed editions will be limited to 250 sets. Please add $2.00 per portfolio for postage and handling. The total price of these portfolios is a tax deductible contribution.

_____unsigned edition(s) $_____

_____signed edition(s) _____

_____postage _____

Total Amount Enclosed $_____

Name   (please print)

Address

City

State   Zip